I DON'T BELIEVE IT!

I DON'T BELIEVE IT!

COMPILED BY
CHRIS BURGESS

ILLUSTRATED BY
BILL TIDY

First published in Great Britain in 1986 by

Octopus Books Limited
59 Grosvenor Street
London W1

ISBN 0 86273 339 1

Illustrations © 1986 Bill Tidy

Printed in Great Britain by
Richard Clay (The Chaucer Press) Ltd
Bungay, Suffolk

Contents

Cops and Robbers

... or the long arm of the law ...

Keeping It in the Family

A woman in Mexico was caught red-handed stealing a juicy piece of meat from her local supermarket. She was marched off to the manager's office to be detained while the police were called. But there was much consternation amongst the staff when the policeman who arrived to arrest her turned out to be none other than her husband. . .

A Rash Porker

A sow and her six piglets were once tried in France on a charge of having killed a child. The defendants were found guilty, and the sow executed. But the defending lawyer managed to get the piglets off with a caution, on the grounds of their extreme youth and the fact that they had been influenced by the bad example of their mother.

Meanwhile, in Switzerland a cockerel was tried for the diabolical crime of laying an egg! Back in the fifteenth century it was believed that a cock's egg in the hands of a witch was evilly potent. The unfortunate rooster was found guilty, sentenced and burned at the stake – along with the egg.

DIY Organ Scholar

Hertfordshire church organists could never be certain that all would be well when they pulled out the stops for a special occasion. There was an outbreak of theft by what the police described as 'an organ nut'. The thief was taking out the pipes – and other bits and pieces – at an alarming rate.

The Rev. Keith Arnold, whose parishes suffered most, was convinced that it was not the work of a scrap thief, who would have taken larger quantities of lead pipes from each organ. He said, 'This can only mean that the parts are being taken by someone wanting to build their own organ.'

Small But Beautiful

In the Western world, more than five million people are engaged in law and its enforcement. (That is the equivalent of the whole population of Scotland.)

Will Rogers, an American noted for his wit and wisdom, said, 'When you read something you can't understand, you can almost be sure it was drawn up by a lawyer.'

In Andorra there is only one lawyer, and he is not allowed to appear in court. In that tiny country this decree was issued in 1864: 'The appearance in our courts of the learned gentlemen of the law, who can make black appear white and white appear black, is forbidden.'

. . . . . An inventor in America worked night and day to develop a foolproof burglar alarm, and almost completed the first model. But then, unfortunately, his laboratory was burgled and the alarm stolen . . . .

The Price of Red Tape

One evening in 1867, a poorly-clad man was shown into Lord Shaftesbury's study in London. The man warned that desperate Irishmen were planning to blow up Clerkenwell Prison.

Lord Shaftesbury believed him and hurried to Whitehall to warn the authorities. They demanded the informant's name and address, which Lord Shaftesbury admitted he was unable to give them.

The authorities then declared, 'There is nothing we can do. We have to disregard any information unless the name and address of the informant are given.'

Clerkenwell Prison was blown up within 24 hours. There were 37 dead and 120 injured.

The Right Place at the Right Time

A wife in Texas had had quite enough of her drunken husband, so she decided to teach him a lesson. She put in an emergency call to the police and requested that they come round immediately.

When the police arrived, she took them into the hall, pointed to her prostrate husband, and demanded that they arrest him. The officers pointed out that there was no law to prevent a man being drunk in his own home. But this failed to satisfy the infuriated wife. She dragged her husband into the street and insisted that the police arrest him there.

Set a Thief to Catch a Thief

The choice of guardians of the law in the 19th century left a lot to be desired.

At Chesham in Buckinghamshire, for example, the man appointed to be constable, thief-taker and peace-officer, was known to have been publicly flogged in Chesham, privately flogged at Aylesbury Gaol, once convicted of stealing lead and once committed to hard labour for assaulting and robbing a boy.

Bumper Hair Harvest

People in a small Oxfordshire village at the end of the last century were robbed of their crowning glory by a wigmaker who used a unique ploy to get his raw materials.

The man, wearing a badge with an authoritative look, called at each house in the village. He announced himself as a Government Barber from London, sent to cut the people's hair for free, as this was the most effective way of avoiding cholera.

So thorough was the trim given to the villagers that they were left almost bald.

Not So Well Read

Nothing went right for would-be robber David Morris. He was passing time before a date with his girlfriend when he wrote a note which said, 'I have got a gun in my pocket and I'll shoot it off unless you hand over the money.'

The amateur thief then went to three shops in London and passed the note over the counter — all with no success. In the first the girl assistant refused to accept the note, believing it contained an obscene suggestion, in the second an Asian assistant shook his head and said he couldn't read English and in the third the shopkeeper explained that he couldn't read the note without his glasses.

Priority for an Old Score

There was considerable excitement at an Irish murder trial when the 'corpse' made a sudden appearance in the court. As the hubbub died down, the judge told the jury to bring in the obvious verdict. The foreman immediately declared that the defendant was guilty.

The bewildered judge bellowed, 'But the murdered man is alive!'

Came the reply, 'Be that as it may. All I know is that the defendant stole my brown mare.'

. . . . . A thief who helped himself to both money and jewellery, told the judge, 'I believe that money alone does not ensure happiness.' . . . .

Gotcha!

Lord Macaulay, the famous historian, was in Rome on holiday. One evening after dinner he decided to take a stroll to the Colosseum. On the way a dark figure in a cloak brushed against him. Soon after, Macaulay found that his watch was missing.

Being no weakling, Macaulay immediately gave chase and overtook his quarry. As communication proved impossible, neither being able to speak the other's language, the encounter ended in a struggle in the semi-darkness, during which the Italian was forced to hand over a watch. Feeling well satisfied with himself, Macaulay walked back to his lodgings.

There, he was greeted by his landlady who said, 'Excuse me, *signor*, I have put your watch on the dressing-table in your room. I found it in the dining-room after you'd gone.'

Tale of a Misspent Youth

Some citizens are so law-abiding that any slight misdemeanour hangs heavily on their conscience for the rest of their lives. One such was a defendant at a Southend court, who was asked if he had had any previous convictions.

The poor soul told the court that once during the war he had been unable to produce his identity card. He had been wearing a bathing costume at the time.

'Wild Bill's A-comin'!'

The last thing Wild Bill Hickock wanted was to be what he became – the greatest gunfighter in the West. It all began when he was accidentally involved in a gunfight in which he shot two roughnecks in self-defence.

Rumour spread quickly in the sensation-hungry West. One printed report stated that Hickock had stood at bay with a six-gun, an Indian knife and a rifle, and fought ten men. When the smoke cleared, all ten lay shot and slashed to death.

Bill tried to deny these stories but people thought he was just being modest. Wherever he went, folk murmured fearfully, 'Wild Bill's a-comin'!' As he became the target for every local killer who hoped to win fame by outgunning this hero, Bill realized that the length of his life depended on his becoming an expert with a gun. And that's what he became, by long hours of hard work and practice.

Bill learned to take other precautions too – like never sitting with his back to the door of a saloon. But one day in 1876 he forgot this golden rule. A roughneck with ambitions to be a famous gunfighter walked into the saloon, spotted his advantage, and pumped lead into Hickock. Wild Bill was dead before his body hit the sawdust-covered floor.

Sand in their Eyes

Twice a week a Belgian riding a bicycle crossed the German border and he always carried a suitcase filled with sand. Each time the customs officials searched the suitcase for contraband, but always in vain.

Sometimes they even emptied all the sand out, expecting to find jewellery, watches or even drugs. But always there was nothing but sand. They racked their brains – what was this Belgian smuggling? He must be selling something over the border!

It was many years later, long after the Belgian had vanished from the scene, that they learned the truth. He had been smuggling . . . bicycles!

On to the Millennium

A 76-year-old man appeared before magistrates in Leeds on his 500th charge of drunkenness. He was given an absolute discharge. But a few days later he turned up for the 501st time. His defence was that he had been celebrating the 500th anniversary.

He was fined 50p.

. . . . . When a golfing judge asked a boy in the witness-box if he understood the nature of an oath, the lad replied, 'Don't I! Aren't I your caddie?' . . . .

One Bad Apple

When Pope Leo XII visited a jail, he insisted on asking every prisoner how he had come to be there. All the prisoners except one protested his innocence. Just one man admitted that he had been rightly convicted.

The Pope turned to the prison superintendent and said, 'Release this rascal at once. I do not wish that his presence should corrupt all these noble gentlemen here!'

If At First You Don't Succeed

A lawsuit in India dragged on for 761 years until it was finally settled in 1966.

The case was first lost in 1205 but the descendants of the plaintiff were a stubborn lot. They just refused to drop it until a judgement was given in their favour.

And their reward? The right to officiate at public functions and precedence at religious festivals.

Shot With His Own Gun

An Australian on an outing into the bush was bitten by a snake. He had no knife to open the wound and drain the poison, so he shot himself in order to bleed the area. Before passing out, he even managed to tie a tourniquet round his arm.

A short time later a group of walkers found him and hurried him off to hospital. He made a good recovery but the happy ending was spoiled when he was visited in hospital by a police detective. He was charged with carrying a firearm on a Sunday and fined £2.

One Law for the Law

A man in Teeside was taken to court for making a two-fingered gesture at a High Court judge in the street. He explained that the gesture had been intended for the mayor. He was acquitted.

An Arm for the Law

A lawyer was defending a man charged with housebreaking. The lawyer stated that his client had merely inserted his arm through a broken window and removed a few articles.

'As my client's arm is not himself,' the lawyer argued, 'I fail to see why the whole individual should be punished because of an offence by one of his limbs.'

The judge thought about this, and said, 'The sentence is one year in prison for the defendant's arm. The defendant can accompany his arm or not, as he chooses.'

The defendant detached his artificial arm, placed it on the desk, and walked from the court.

A Mugger Mugged

A attempted street robbery ended up with an intended victim being charged with the killing of the assailant.

The accused told the court that the deceased had ordered him to hand over his wife's purse. The purse was in a basket on the ground. So he bent down, put his hands up his wife's skirt, detached her wooden leg, and battered the assailant on the head with it.

I'VE GOT MEN OUT SEARCHING FOR THE WEAPON

Twelve Good Persons and True

A murder trial in America ended before it began, during the swearing in of the jury. One of the jurymen asked the judge to speak louder because he was very deaf.

Investigation of the jury revealed that another man, who was stone deaf, thought the trial had something to do with divorce; three could not understand English; and another had come to the court for a gun licence.

Shome Mishtake Surely?

Printed in the *Ely Standard*:

'We apologize for the error in last week's paper in which we stated that Mr Arnold Dogbody was a defective in the police force. This was a typographical error. We meant, of course, that Mr Dogbody is a detective in the police farce and we are sorry for any embarrassment caused.'

Indecent Exposure

It's not often that a burglar asks the police for help, especially when he's on a job. But sometimes there are extenuating circumstances . . .

In this particular case the wily villain had been trying to break through a skylight into a supermarket but found that either he was too big or it was too small. So he took off his clothes and tried again – throwing everything down into the shop below him. But finally he was forced to admit defeat – and was left standing stark naked on the roof of the store.

It was then that he shouted for help, and a passing policeman obliged. After all, at least it was warm in the cell!

Not So Horny

A thief who stole a rhino horn – believed in the Far East to be an aphrodisiac – from a Brighton museum failed to find his sex life pepped up much . . . it had been treated with a harmful chemical preservative.

Long Arm of the Law

From a US college magazine: 'The British legal system is the best in the world. Each case is tried with scrupulous fairness and justice is not only done, it is seen to be done. There are no inflexible rules: the law is elastic.' Which is why some people get longer stretches than others.

. . . . . A British judge went to great pains to explain the rules of insanity to a jury. When the verdict on the case was returned, the foreman said, 'We are all of one mind – insane.' . . . .

Enough's Enough

The jury had been out for hours, and the judge was growing impatient. A young man was charged with the savage murder of both parents, and it seemed obvious to everyone that he was guilty.

The judge recalled the jury and asked if he could give them any further guidance. The foreman declined, saying that they understood the evidence very clearly. The jury continued to deliberate.

Hours passed, and the jury finally returned with a verdict of 'Not guilty'. There was a gasp in the court and the judge almost exploded. Forgetting himself, he fumed, 'But we all know the prisoner's guilty and should hang!'

The foreman said, 'That's the trouble, My Lord. We don't doubt the prisoner's guilt, but don't you think there have been enough deaths in that family lately?'

A Sad Case of Self-Destruction

A man in Bangkok informed police that his watch had been stolen, and that he knew who had taken it. The informant believed that the thief had been on the wanted list for some months.

He told the police where the criminal could be found, and he even gave them a photograph to help with identification.

The police carried out a raid, shots were fired, and one man was killed. Alas, he turned out to be the informer. The police apologized to his family, but explained that he had sent them a photograph of himself by mistake.

. . . . . A woman convicted of killing her husband with a kitchen knife applied for a widow's allowance. The application was refused . . . .

Devil Women

In the Book of Exodus in the Bible, it says, 'Thou shalt not suffer a witch to live.' It was this sentence that inspired Pope Innocent VIII to create the Inquisition, an organization of men with the authority to imprison, convict and punish those guilty of witchcraft.

Ways of determining whether or not a woman was a witch were bizarre. Suspects were first examined by an experienced witchfinder. He searched the woman's body for a 'devil's bite'. This was any mark on the body that experienced no pain, or showed no blood when pricked with a needle or knife.

Another form of trial was to tie the woman's legs together, and throw her into deep water. If she floated, then she was considered guilty. If she sank, she was innocent.

During the three hundred years from 1484, the Christian Church put to death 300,000 women convicted of witchcraft.

That Guilty Feeling

A defendant in a closely contested case was unable to attend court because of illness. The verdict was in his favour, so his solicitor sent him a cable which read: 'Justice has triumphed!'

To which the client replied, 'We must appeal at once!'

Dummy

Magistrates ruled that a Scotsman acted in the public interest when he leapt into a shop front and wrestled with a tailor's dummy early one New Year's Day.

The Scot had been charged with housebreaking, but his defence was that he had heard a crash of glass from a shop and had seen two men running away. He also thought he saw a third man through the plate-glass window. There was a large hole in the glass, he explained, so he jumped through it and landed on the tailor's dummy.

It was at this point that the police arrested him.

The Law is an Ass

In 1819 the penalty for impersonating a Chelsea pensioner was death.

In Quebec, Canada, it is illegal to sell anti-freeze to Indians.

In Minnesota, USA, it is against the law to hang male and female underwear on the same line.

In Saskatchewan, USA, you must not drink water in a beer parlour.

In El Paso, Texas, all public buildings must be equipped with 'spittoons of a kind and number to efficiently contain expectorations into them . . . '

A transportation law in Texas: 'When two trains approach each other at a crossing, they should both stop, and neither shall start up until the other has gone.'

In Waterloo, Nebraska, it is illegal for a barber to eat onions between 7 a.m. and 7 p.m.

The Council of Widnes, Lancashire, introduced a fine of £5 for those who made a habit of falling asleep in the reading rooms of the libraries.

But good news from Ohio! 'A person assaulted or lynched by a mob may recover from the county in which the assault is made, a sum not exceeding five hundred dollars.'

..... *A police sergeant who found that the licence on his dog had expired took out a summons against himself* ....

Out on a Spree

The richest bonus ever enjoyed by the criminal fraternity of London was the Great Smog of 1952. Under cover of the choking smog blanket which lasted for three weeks, thieves went on the spree of a lifetime. The looting of shops and other properties for rich pickings was so widespread that the police, unable to move speedily around the city, were almost helpless.

Lamb to the Slaughter

A handsome sheepskin coat hanging in the cloakroom of an hotel in Bognor Regis took the eye of a youth with few scruples. Wearing his booty, he hitched a lift from a passing coach.

He found to his horror that the passengers were all detective inspectors on their way home from a conference on crime. The thief made himself small and hoped for the best.

But his luck was out. One of the detectives began taking an interest in the coat, and finally identified it as his own.

The thief was dropped off at the nearest police station.

..... *One result of the prohibition of alcoholic drinks in the United States, 1920-1933, was that in one year the number of drinking places in New York doubled* ....

Drinking and Driving Made Easy

A police car was patrolling the M1 late one evening, when the officers saw a Rolls Royce parked on the hard shoulder, with a man slumped against it on the far side.

They pulled over and asked the man if he had been drinking. When he admitted that he had, they immediately breathalysed him and found him well over the limit. After some disagreement as to which officer should drive the Rolls back to the station, one of them went across to the driver's seat – only to find that sitting patiently inside was the chauffeur.

. . . . . A drinks extension until midnight was granted by local magistrates to an Oxfordshire hotel, where there was a dinner-dance organized by Alcoholics Anonymous . . . .

There's Life in the Old Dog Yet

A notorious brothel in South Carolina was raided by the police, and dozens of clients were charged. The police were inundated with phone calls from men trying to get their names taken off the charge sheet.

But they also received a request from one elderly man who offered a bribe to have his name *added* to the list.

Way Out

... or there's nowt so strange as folk ...

Making a Meal of Communication

One problem with the first military tanks was communication between tank crews and the Infantry. The crude radio transmitters and receivers proved useless, because of the ear-shattering noise of the tank's engine.

So, two carrier pigeons were kept in each tank. Messages were to be written on rice paper and attached to the pigeon's leg. However, in the heat of battle, more than one tank commander forgot to send these messages and, rather than admit it, chose pigeon pie as a tasty way of destroying the evidence.

Old Habits Die Hard

Drawing attention to yourself when you're a fugitive on the run is not a good idea. Ignoring this simple rule cost the Marquis de Condonset his head during the French Revolution.

Disguised as a peasant, this foolish worthy strode into an inn full of half-starved (real) peasants, and called in a loud voice, 'Make me an omelette with a dozen eggs.'

General Chaos

Count Suverov was the greatest Russian general of the 18th century – and the oddest. Instead of mustering his troops with a bugle call, he summoned them personally by crowing like a cock.

His normal habit was to go to bed in the afternoon, and rise in the middle of the night. He slept on hay on the ground, rather than in a comfortable bed, and when he rode about on horseback, he wore only a shirt. And, most confusing of all to his loyal men, his orders were always issued in rhyme.

Means to an End

A blind man was standing at a crossroads in a town in Scotland, when a dog walked up to him and relieved himself down his trouser leg. To the astonishment of a passer-by, the blind man took out a biscuit from his pocket and offered it to the dog. This so impressed the passer-by that he congratulated the blind man on his kindness to animals.

The blind man replied, 'Not at all. I was only trying to find which end his mouth was, so that I could kick the other end.'

. . . . . Madame Tallien, who was a member of the French Court during the reign of Louis XIV, bathed in crushed strawberries when they were available . . . .

Trumpets on the Wing

Latin tempers frayed and passengers were on the point of mutiny aboard a plane delayed for three hours at Madrid airport. Tough Civil Guards, armed with machine guns, were even summoned to quell the unrest.

It was then that Ray Simmonds, principal trumpet player of the Royal Philharmonic Orchestra from London decided a little light music was called for. So he took out his instrument and began to play – 'Viva Espana'.

Do Not Walk on the Grass

In the London suburb of Wimbledon in 1887, a fashionable entertainment was to pay a visit to Coleman's Circus – even though it consisted of only one man and his horse. The fascinating thing was that this horse wore rubber boots, and spent its time pulling rollers and mowers on grass tennis courts.

The rubber-booted horse was the brainchild of Thomas Coleman, the first full-time groundsman appointed by the All England Croquet and Lawn Tennis Club. Coleman took his job very seriously, and he didn't want the courts in his charge ruined by iron horseshoes.

Coleman remained with the famous club for forty years, and made the courts the finest in the world.

Management Tips

Lenten sermons at St Andrew-by-the-Wardrobe parish church in the City of London have been tailored to local tastes. They are being billed as: Start-up Schemes, Business Expansion, Profit and Loss and, finally, The Balance Sheet.

Noah's Ark on Mont Blanc

In 1960 an Italian doctor announced that the world would end at 3.00 p.m. on 14th July. He predicted earthquakes, floods and great tidal waves. The good news was that survival was possible, but only high on Mont Blanc in the Alps.

The doctor invited others to join him in building a house on the mountain, and a total of 70 people joined the project, some of them using all their life savings.

Soon after noon on the 14th, the doctor bought a one-way ticket for the cable-car that ran up the mountain. He was joined on the journey by his fellow-investors and a number of tourists, curious to see what would happen. Three o'clock came and went – and nothing happened. The tourists outside the house laughed and jeered. At last the front door opened, and the doctor emerged.

He said, 'Anyone can make a mistake, and you should be grateful that I have.'

Not in Front of the Children

A chief sugar boiler in a seaside rock factory pioneered a unique form of protest. He was fed up with his working conditions and the responsibility of making some 20,000 sticks of rock a day. So instead of the usual 'Torbay', 'Bournemouth' or 'Brighton' running all the way through, he turned out 1,000 sticks bearing a word that has more to do with snooker than with the seaside . . .

The Biter Bit

What would Barbara Woodhouse say? A breeder of dogs has been censured by the Kennel Club, of which she is a member, for her unusual training methods. It seems that the lady believes that the punishment should fit the crime, for when one of her dogs bit a passer-by, she bit the dog.

Strictly for the Birds

The Rev. Favell Hopkins of Huntingdon was a rich man, but so miserly that he denied himself the basic necessities of life.

One Sunday morning, on his way to church, he noticed a scarecrow in a field. The Rev. Hopkins took off its hat, examined it carefully, and then compared it with his own. Deciding that the advantage lay with the scarecrow's hat, he placed it on his head, put his own on the scarecrow, and continued his journey.

. . . . . A café in Bridport, Dorset, displayed this notice in the window: 'Closed for lunch. Open 2.00 p.m.' . . . .

Nil All!

A small but select band of politicians in Britain share the doubtful honour of having scored no votes in an election.

The pioneer was Lord Garvagh, Liberal candidate for Reigate in 1832, who managed to avoid making himself popular with a single member of the electorate. Seven years later, another Liberal, L. Oliphant, repeated the achievement.

In 1841 the Liberal monopoly was broken by a notable double, in which two Chartist Party candidates scored zero. The Chartists went ahead in 1847 with a candidate for Tiverton. But their nil-vote supremacy heralded the end of the party, which went out of business a few years later.

This left the field open to the Conservative Party, which notched up a nought with Viscount Lascelles at Tewkesbury. Not to be outdone, the Liberals failed to score in the same constituency twelve years later. The last of this distinguished band, F. R. Lees, achieved total unpopularity in an 1860 by-election.

The list stops there – but only because candidates may now vote for themselves!

It's Never Too Late

Waldomiro da Silva was born in 1867 – 21 years before slavery was abolished in Brazil. In 1986 he married . . . at the age of 119. His sweetheart was a mere 65.

The elaborate ceremony was organized by the great grandson of da Silva's former slave master.

LOOKS LIKE THEY BROUGHT
BACK SLAVERY

She Sells Sea-shells by the Seashore

But who was the 'she' in that well-known tongue-twister? She was Mary Anning, who lived at Lyme Regis on the coast of Dorset in the 19th century.

Mary and her father made a living by collecting and selling sea-shells and fossils. When Mary was only eleven, her father died, but the young girl carried on the business alone.

Then Mary found a giant fossil about 10 metres long. It was new to scientists, for it was the remains of a creature that lived a hundred million years ago. They called it Ichthyosaurus.

Further discoveries followed, so important that Mary was given a grant by the government – a rare event even in those days. She died aged 48. In a church in Lyme Regis there is a stained-glass window to her memory. And at the British Museum you can see a portrait of her, beside one of her greatest discoveries, the Plesiosaur.

Under False Pretences

A vicar gave a lady in his parish a birthday present of a Bible. She asked him to write his name in it. He did so, inscribing it as a gift 'from the author'.

Amazing Grace

Job opportunities for women were few and far between on the west coast of Ireland in the 16th century. But that didn't worry Grace O'Malley. She became a pirate chief of outstanding success. From Clew Bay she preyed on ships in the Atlantic.

Much of her youth was spent on pirate ships and when she became a captain, a small but fierce fleet was brought under her control. Though arrested a few times, Grace was never brought to trial and she retired happily in 1586 at fifty years of age to enjoy her loot.

The Result was a Draw

In 1808 two Frenchmen fought a duel half-a-mile above the gardens of the Tuileries. But instead of firing at each other, they used blunderbusses to blast away at the hot air balloon below which each was suspended.

Simultaneous hits occurred, and both balloons plummeted to earth, killing their occupants.

Stairs are Safer

Instructions abroad don't always tell the visitor exactly what they want to know...

A lift in a hotel in Madrid advised with confidence: 'To move the cabin, push button of wishing floor. If the cabin should enter more persons, each one should press number of wishing floor. Driving is then going alphabetically by natural order. Button retaining pressed position shows received command for visiting station.' *Olé.*

Budget Day Thoughts

'... the rapacity and greed of the Government go beyond all limits. It is now actually proposing to place a tax on incomes.

'Those with £100 to £105 a year are to pay a 1/40th part, and above £200, 1/10th. This is a vile Jacobin jumped-up jack-in-the-box office impertinence. Is a true Briton to have no privacy? Are the fruits of his labour and toil to be picked over, farthing by farthing, by pimply minions of bureaucracy?'

A familiar complaint – except this one was written by John Knyveton, a naval surgeon at the time of Nelson, dated 12 January 1799.

Sweet Smell of Success

Dudley Taw, of Cleveland, Ohio, recently concocted a cologne for men designed to promote its user to a position of great wealth and power.

The cologne is called 'CEO', which stands for Chief Executive Officer. For the man who wants to smell like the boss. . .

. . . . . *Printed on the inside cover of a theological work: 'Spread the word of the Lord. No part of this book may be reproduced without permission from the publishers.'* . . . .

Measure for Measure

Sir Francis Galton, who lived in the later part of the 19th century, was addicted to measuring, counting and analysing statistics.

One of his numerous projects was to gather material for a Beauty Map of Great Britain. Every woman he saw he classified as beautiful, middling or ugly. His general conclusion was that London had the prettiest girls and Aberdeen the ugliest. Another finding was that the finest men came from Ballater in Scotland.

Galton extended his research to Africa, for he had great admiration for the figures of the native women. Some misunderstandings occurred when he tried to use a tape-measure on them. So he devised a way of measuring hips and busts using a sextant.

Other projects included 'The weights of British noblemen during the last three generations', and he wrote a fact-filled paper on 'Three generations of lunatic cats'. He even set out to measure the honesty of nations. Not surprisingly he concluded that the British were top of the league. He declared that Salonika in Greece was 'the centre of gravity of lying'.

In the end Galton tried to persuade people to breed selectively – like racehorses – and produce a super race. He failed completely – people just went on doing what came naturally. . .

Beyond Belief

In Europe, yogurt is yogurt, and it is not difficult to believe that it is yogurt because it tastes like it. In the USA, things are not so simple.

There, a company called This Can't Be Yogurt, which patently is a yogurt company because it sells frozen dollops of the stuff, announced that it was floating off 505,000 of its shares. It was promptly sued by another company entitled I Can't Believe It's Yogurt, which is equally involved in the trade, owning a number of frozen yogurt stores.

I Can't Believe It's Yogurt claimed that This Can't Be Yogurt was a trade mark which infringed its own – and it asked for at least $750,000 in compensatory and punitive damages.

The Sport of Wings

Airmen on both sides in World War One often behaved more like rival sportsmen than deadly enemies. When the greatest German air ace of the war, Baron von Richthofen, known as the 'Red Baron' was shot down, Allied airmen buried him with full military honours.

Hell's Bells! We'll Sue

Hell's Angels sued their next-door neighbours . . . for giving them a bad name! The bike gang hit the roof when the McSorley family accused the Angels of forcing them to flee their £75,000 house at Windsor, Berks. And they blew a gasket when the local valuation court cut Mrs Pat McSorley's rates from £337 a year to a nominal £1.

'We are not nightmare neighbours. Our solicitors are taking action over this family's claims, and we will do battle in the court,' said a Hell's Angel spokesman. Mrs McSorley, 42, told of week-long parties, sword and gun-toting bikers, noisy motorbikes . . . and of Angels exposing themselves to her. 'This woman lives in a dream world,' said the Angels.

You Can't Take It With You

An old Lancashire man knew he was dying. Not long before the end he told his wife that he wanted to change his will, and summoned his lawyer.

The solicitor arrived and sat by the old man's bed. The dying man said, 'In the last few years I have become convinced that when I die, I will be reborn on this earth. I now believe firmly in reincarnation. Please change my will – I wish to leave everything to myself.'

CONGRATULATIONS. YOU'VE JUST BECOME THE RICHEST FLY IN THE WORLD!

Which End Up?

Confused by modern art? Try standing on your head.

'Le Bateau' by Matisse was hung upside down in New York's Museum of Modern Art for forty-seven days – and nobody noticed!

For Richer, For Poorer

A rich New York tailor went to extraordinary lengths to make sure that his money was left to the poor of the city.

In his will he stipulated that over seventy pairs of old trousers should be auctioned off, and that the proceeds should go to the needy of the city. The sting in the tail, though, was a paragraph in the will which stated: 'I desire that these garments shall in no way be examined or meddled with, but be disposed of as they are found at the time of my death, and no purchaser to buy more than one pair.'

The trousers were duly sold off to those not too choosy about their choice of garment – all at knock-down prices. Much to their surprise, all the pockets were found to be stitched up. And when they opened them they found the real legacy of the will – each pair of trousers contained a thousand dollars in banknotes!

Tour de France

The celebrations for the fortieth anniversary of D-Day included a series of mini-trips of the battle zone. One of these involved overnight travel on the ferry to France and then a day spent whizzing to the invasion beaches, Pegasus, Gold, Sword, June and Arromanches, together with side trips to Honfleur and Bayeaux, before collapsing back on board.

That package was called The Longest Day.

. . . . . In the parish of Chingford, Essex, is Friday-Hill House, in which King Charles knighted a loin of beef on an oak table . . . .

Where There's a Will . . .

Here are some unusual clauses from a selection of eccentric wills:

'The undertaker's fees come to nothing, as I won them from him at a game of billiards.'

'I leave my lawyer, Hubert Lewis, the task of explaining to my relatives why they didn't get a million dollars apiece.'

'To my wife Anna (who is no damn good) I leave one dollar.'

'I direct that all my creditors be paid, except my landlord.'

'To my wife I leave her lover, and the knowledge that I wasn't the fool she thought I was.'

'To my chauffeur, I leave my cars. He almost ruined them, and I want him to have the satisfaction of finishing the job.'

HI EVERYBODY. THIS IS HUBERT SPEAKING FROM THE YACHT. YOU DIDN'T GET THE MONEY BECAUSE I DID!

Candidate for the Green Party?

Lord Rokeby, who was born in 1713, was way ahead of his time when he constructed a solar-heated bath-house on his estate near Hythe in Kent. He bathed several times a day, refused to drink anything but water, substituted honey for sugar, and would not eat products based on wheat.

When he inherited his estate, the land was fertile and well-cultivated. Lord Rokeby put a stop to all that. He ordered that the fields should be allowed to go back to wilderness, and that no tree or hedge should be chopped or even pruned. All the grounds, including the walled ornamental gardens, were opened up, so that the horses, sheep and cattle could wander at will.

In the decaying coach-house, the family carriages were left to rot, for Lord Rokeby walked almost everywhere. When he walked to the beach for a swim, a carriage followed him – not for himself, but in case the servants got tired.

For a time he was MP for Canterbury. But the party politics of the House of Commons so disgusted him that he told his constituents that he no longer felt able to represent them.

At the age of 87, feeling that death was near, he summoned his nephew, who was to inherit his fortune. When the nephew wanted to call a doctor, the old man warned him that if he did, and the doctor failed to kill him, he would use his last strength to cut the young man out of his will.

And when he died, his wild estates were prospering.

Shalom way To Go

The inflation in Israel is running at 60%, so when a tourist decided to go there for his holiday, he rang first to enquire about hotel prices. When he asked about the nightly cost of a room, the receptionist replied, 'It depends how soon you get here.'

Gold Bricks

Australia's latest gold strike is right in the city of Perth. At the State Mint to be precise.

Officials say that about 1,000 ounces of gold, which vaporized during the mint's 86-year history of refining, has impregnated the building and is to be recovered.

Mind you, to get the gold – worth A$500,000 – the buildings of the mint will have to be demolished and the walls and ceilings smelted. But the mint's processes are to be moved to a new site anyway. The golden windfall will go towards the cost.

The Very Conservative MP

The most conservative MP who ever lived was a Colonel Sibthorp, member for Lincoln from 1826. He was opposed to all changes, all innovations and all foreigners.

Indeed Sibthorp accused Queen Victoria of making a ghastly mistake in marrying a foreigner, declaring that Prince Albert's character was permanently damaged by his foreign birth. So while Sibthorp was MP for Lincoln, Queen Victoria refused to visit the city.

The Great Exhibition of 1851 was inspired by Prince Albert. The Colonel denounced it as 'one of the greatest humbugs, one of the greatest frauds, one of the greatest absurdities ever known!'

He believed it was designed to bring waves of foreigners to England's shores and warned the locals: 'Take care of your wives and daughters, take care of your property and your lives!'

But in one respect Colonel Sibthorp was way ahead of his time. He cunningly suggested that foreign travel should be curtailed by limiting the amount of currency that could be taken abroad.

Bookworm

Richard Heber ended his life as a recluse gloating over his treasures behind the shutters of his house in Pimlico. The treasures were – books!

As a child of eight Richard catalogued the vast library he had already accumulated in his father's house. When his father, a rich clergyman, died and left his fortune to Richard, the book-buying exploits became fantastic.

Rooms, cupboards, passages and corridors of his house became choked with books. Books were piled up to the very ceiling. When one house was stuffed with them, he bought another and began stuffing that. Once he took time off to propose marriage to a Miss Richardson Currer of Yorkshire, a well-known book-collector; it would have been a marriage of libraries but negotiations broke down.

When the Richard Heber estate was investigated after his death in 1883, trustees found one mansion in Cheshire, two houses in London, and houses in Paris, Brussels, Antwerp, Ghent and Germany – all crammed with books!

..... A Turkish student in Japan demanded that the name of the communal hot bathing places be changed from 'toruko' (meaning Turkish bath), as the naughty goings on there demeaned the honour of his nation. They are now called 'soopurando' (soapland) instead . . . .

A Head for Business

Enterprising Gary Mason decided to get ahead in the world – by selling advertising space on his head. He shaved off all his hair, and offered companies the space – any message painted on for £30.

Said optimistic Gary, 'I'm surprised nobody thought of it before.'

Till Death Do Us Part

. . . or love and marriage . . .

A Bride By Any Other Name

A couple of young farmers decided to get married on the same day. Before applying for the licences, however, they celebrated so thoroughly that by mistake they each gave the name of the other's intended bride.

As neither of them could read, it was left to the clergyman to discover the error on the day planned for the weddings. Rather than disappoint their friends, who were looking forward to the festivities, all four participants agreed to be paired as the licences decreed.

Like Father, Like Son

A teacher in Hull in Humberside sent a boy home because of his smell. When the lad returned to school the following day — no cleaner — he had a note from his mother.

It informed the teacher that Harold smelled the same as his father, and that his dad smelled just fine. As proof of this, the mother added that she had lived with Harold's dad for 25 years, and she should know.

Happiness Is A Waterworks Bill

Divorce has not always been the simple process it is today. One unhappy spouse went to the lengths of including provision for his own divorce in a special Act of Parliament.

He was a town clerk, and he sought his future happiness via a municipal Waterworks Bill. As he was in charge of drafting the bill, he wrote in a somewhat unusual clause.

The Royal Assent was granted to the bill, the town got its water supply, and the Town Clerk got his freedom. The extra clause stated, quite simply, ' . . . and the Town Clerk's marriage is hereby dissolved.'

Cornet Duet

A repentant wife admitted to her husband that she had committed adultery with the owner of an ice-cream cart. She agreed to write a farewell letter to her lover, and the husband insisted on delivering it in person.

When the two men met, they shook hands and had a friendly chat. Then the husband returned home to his wife with two free ice-cream cornets.

The Language of Love

A young Frenchman experienced a set-back and a slap in the face when he attempted to woo an English girl with words. His intentions were honourable, but his command of English was less than perfect. He meant to say, 'When I look at you, time stands still.' What he actually said was, 'Your face would stop a clock.'

Making the Most of It

These epitaphs appear on tombstones:

In loving memory of
SYDNEY WILLIAM SMYTHE
1898-1951
Cherished by his wife
Rest in Peace – until we meet again

In remembrance of
NICHOLAS TOKE
He married five wives whom he survived.
At the age of 93 he walked to London
to seek a sixth but died before he
found her.

Bedtime Stories

In his various palaces, Louis XIV of France had 413 beds. All were elaborately carved, gilded and hung with costly embroideries. His great joy was the magnificent bed in the Palace of Versailles, on which was woven in gold the words, 'The Triumph of Venus'. But when Louis married his second wife, who was a religious bigot, she had the pagan subject replaced by 'The Sacrifice of Abraham'.

Battered Wives Trek to Cheltenham

In the mid-1960s, a judge in Sheffield said that cruelty in marriage had to be assessed according to social background.

M'Lud's comments were made during a hearing on wife-beating. He argued that 'in some parts of England' a little thumping on a Saturday night might not amount to cruelty. On the other hand, his Lordship considered that the same carry-on in, for example, Cheltenham, would no doubt be an act of cruelty.

One . . . Two . . . Tree

Hindu men sometimes marry a tree – as a way of avoiding bad luck. They believe it is unlucky to marry three times, so, if a man wants to take a third bride, he marries a tree first. Then he burns it down, and this frees him to marry the woman of his choice.

All the Same in the Dark

When the love that Darsun Yilmaz of Damali on the Black Sea wanted to lavish on his neighbour's daughter was spurned, he opted for abduction. In August 1972, the yearning lover turned up in his beloved's garden at midnight with a ladder. He climbed into the bedroom, threw a blanket over her head, and bundled her into his car. Whispering endearments, he unwrapped the package, drooling at the thought of his first kiss.

But the wriggling female form was not what he expected. It was the girl's 91-year-old granny, who clouted him good and hard.

I DON'T THINK THIS IS YOUR CAR EITHER!

Third Time Lucky

During a case of bigamy in a Dublin court, a long tale of complicated relationships and deceptions was unfolded on the part of the defendant. The judge lectured the man, expressing his horror at what had been revealed.

But the defendant was unabashed. 'Sure, your lordship,' he said, 'wasn't I only tryin' hard to get a good one?'

A Lean Woman, Much Kissed . . .

If you want a slim, trim figure and are not too worried about your life span, then the recipe is kissing, and plenty of it.

Researchers in America claim that your heartbeat accelerates when you kiss, and that each kiss reduces the length of your life by three minutes. But the good news is that each kiss uses up three calories; to lose a stone, all you have to do is kiss 14,000 times.

Blind Love

Blind Jack of Knaresborough walked the 250 miles from London to his home in Yorkshire with just one thought in his mind – Dolly Benson. He wanted to get back to the love he had left behind when he had paid his once-in-a-lifetime visit to the capital.

But there was a shock for him on arrival. Dolly's parents had forced her to become engaged to a shoemaker, and the wedding was timed for the following morning. Blind though he was, Jack went into action.

Guided by a friend, Jack climbed a ladder to the window of Dolly's bedroom that night. Dolly was more than willing, and the pair eloped, while her parents snored peacefully. The happy couple were married the following morning, had four healthy children, and lived happily ever after.

Exit the Late Departed

The playground of a primary school in Liverpool is beside a cemetery, so that there were times when the children could watch and hear a funeral from a short distance.

One day the headmaster spotted a group of the younger children playing funerals. They had dug a hole, and one of them lowered a shoe box into it. As this was being done, another child said, in a sad voice, 'In the name of the Father, and of the Son, and into the hole he goes.'

. . . . . Lord Goddard, a former Lord Chancellor, ruled that divorce, not murder, was the correct way of getting rid of an unfaithful wife . . . .

A Problem for the Fish

The wife of a famous film star had numerous rows with her husband, mainly because he spent all his spare time fishing.

Soon after one of these domestic upheavals, one of her husband's cronies called at the house and asked where he was.

'Go down to the bridge,' said the wife, drily, 'and look around until you see a pole with a worm at each end of it.'

Staying Married the Hard Way

So desperate was one woman to get a divorce that she mobilized three male friends to drag her husband into bed with a strange woman. The plan was to photograph proof of 'adultery'.

The trap was sprung and the husband frog-marched into the bedroom. There a frantic struggle ensued, during which the husband smashed the camera and escaped. To prevent any replay of the incident, he joined the army.

Limited Bliss

Kathryn Sluckin changed her mind about marriage within an hour of being wed. She married Jerzy Sluckin at Kensington Register Office in November 1975 and the reception was in full swing when Kathryn decided that she wasn't sure the man was for her. She announced, 'It won't work!' and vanished.

Her husband later traced her to the Divine Light Meditation Commune in Finchley, where she was living happily without him.

'Loverly' Day

Why lovers send cards to each other on the feast day of St Valentine is something of a mystery. All we know about the saint is that he was a Roman dignitary who was clubbed to death for helping persecuted Christians.

Whatever the origins, the idea has caught on to the tune of between seven and eight million Valentine cards in Britain *alone*. It seems that more women buy cards, but the men who do spend fifty % more on a card.

One of the world's biggest spenders, Greek millionaire Aristotle Onassis, once lashed out £180,000 on a Valentine card for opera star, Maria Callas. The card was studded with diamonds and emeralds, and was delivered in no ordinary envelope – the wrapping was a black mink coat.

Marx Sparks

Chico Marx, one of the world-famous Marx brothers, was caught by his wife kissing a chorus girl. Tempers flared, and Mrs Marx demanded an explanation.

Unable to deny the evidence, the best Chico could do was, 'I wasn't kissing her. I was just whispering in her mouth.'

Woolly, Weedy, Weaky

Even Latin lovers have their wooing difficulties, and one such was Paco Vila, a student from Madrid. Paco was crazy about big English women, but they scorned his weedy frame, for he weighed-in at only seven stone.

So Paco made up his weight by wearing woolly jumpers beneath his shirt. Thus clad he sallied forth to a discotheque, where fortune smiled on his new-found bulk. An English girl who had abandoned her diet for the holiday consented to dance with him. Paco was in his seventh heaven, until a particularly energetic rumba began to weaken his overburdened body. The crisis came when, at the end of the dance, the English girl stroked his cheek. It was too much for poor Paco, who keeled over in a dead faint.

When they examined him at the hospital, he was wearing 17 woolly sweaters.

. . . . . *Was Ethelred the Unready, one of England's least-loved kings, living up to his name on his wedding night? He was found in bed with both his bride and his mother-in-law!* . . . .

A Flight on the Side

In the early days of flying, when people were wary of this new form of travel, a promotion man hit on the idea of giving free flights to the wives of businessmen who had booked seats.

The idea was welcomed, and the airline kept a record of the names of those who took advantage of the offer. Some time later, a letter was sent to the wives, asking if they had enjoyed the trip.

Unfortunately, a large percentage of them replied, 'What aeroplane trip?'

. . . . . When Lord Chief Justice Russell was asked what the penalty was for bigamy, he replied, 'Two mothers-in-law.' . . . .

Recorded Delivery

A German wife sacrificed her freedom as a result of last-minute weakness.

The day before the divorce hearing, she had gone to her husband's office to discuss the division of their property. Even at that late stage, her husband pleaded that the proceedings should be called off.

In court the wife was resolute – there would be no reconciliation as far as she was concerned. In backing her case she told the judge that she and her husband had not made love for eighteen months.

'It's a lie!' shouted the husband. 'We made love only yesterday in my office.'

The wife hotly denied it, but her husband replied, 'I can prove it. I managed to mark her bottom with the office date-stamp.'

And he had . . .

Just Listen, Darling!

In a bar in America, the most popular record on the juke-box was a novelty number in which the only sound to be heard was a typewriter. The record was played every time a drinker who was supposed to be working late at the office phoned home ...

..... A correction was necessary in a printing of the Bible which included the line: 'Greater love hath no man than this, that he lay down his wife for his friends.' ....

Love Is ...

Just in case you are in any doubt about what love is, here is the definition according to the First International Conference of Love and Attraction:

> 'The cognitive-affective state characterized by intrusive and obsessive fantasizing concerning reciprocity of amorant feeling by the object of the amorance.'

..... A defendant in a divorce case claimed ignorance of the true meaning of adultery. He said, 'I did not think it was adultery during the daytime.' ....

Long-Standing Engagement

A couple of lovers in Mexico City did not believe in making hasty decisions. Octavio Guillen and Adriana Martinez were engaged 67 years before finally getting married in 1969. On the big day they were both 82.

Encore

Getting married and staying married was not good enough for Jack and Edna Moran of Seattle, USA. Since the original and perfectly legal ceremony in 1937, they have renewed their vows no less than 40 times. Places in which they have been wed include Cairo, Egypt, and Westminster Abbey, London.

Sitting Pretty

Not content with its well-earned reputation for automobile engineering the German car-maker BMW is now trying its hand at a spot of social engineering.

Careful research by the company has decided them that few things irritate a driver more than to find that the driving seat has been moved from his or her favourite position by another driver. And wives are the parties most likely to be held guilty of that offence when the husband jumps into the family car in the morning – already late for work.

So BMW has started to offer with its more expensive models an electronically-controlled seat which 'remembers' the driver's usual seating position.

. . . . . A young Oxford couple married in the very same church where they were christened together 24 years before . . . .

Social Register

Eighteenth-century parish registers were just as keen on publishing 'human interest' stories as any of today's newspapers. This one is dated 1 June 1787.

'Anecdote – When the Rev. John Clark, late master of Charter-House in Hull, was curate at St Trinity there, four couples were married by him at the same time, and the following odd circumstances attended each:

With regard to the first couple, the bridegroom had forgot to bring a ring, in consequence of which he was obliged to borrow one; the bride of the second had lost that finger upon which the ring is commonly put.

A man shaking the iron gates leading into the choir, said aloud that the third bride already had a husband and with regard to the fourth, one of the bridesmaids begged the parson, for God's sake to be quick, as the bride was in labour.'

Manly Pursuit

The Canadians are finding that while good intentions about not offending any conceivable minority grouping sound fine and dandy they can prove difficult to put into practice.

A new and impressive museum was built across the Ottawa river from Parliament Hill. From the beginning the project had been given a working title: the National Museum of Man.

But the very idea of calling it anything like that in modern non-sexist Canada caused consternation, both in and out of parliament. A national search for a name acceptable to all Canadians, yet still describing the museum's proper function, was instituted.

The museum authorities came up with more than 50 names, including the Museum of Man and Woman, the Museum of Mankind, and the Museum of People. More original were some of the ideas from the public, who wrote in with nearly 2000 ideas. Proposals included the Museum of Herstory and History, the Museum of Men, Women and Gays, the Museum of Man and his Wife and the National Museum of Others.

. . . . . In his will a husband left his wife, 'One pair of trousers, free of duty and carriage paid, as a symbol of what she wanted to wear in my lifetime'. . . . .

Technical Tales

EMERGENCY
STARTING
BOOT

. . . or lies, damned lies and statistics . . .

Repeats from Space?

In 1953, in the days before satellites bounced television signals round the world, viewers in Britain rubbed their eyes when the identification card and call letters of TV station KLEE in Texas, USA, appeared on their screens.

BBC engineers contacted KLEE, and were astonished to learn that the station had been off the air for three years! The picture seen in Britain must have originated in Texas, but where had it been meanwhile? And why was it seen only in Britain? Do TV signals hang about in space, waiting for the chance of yet another repeat?

Oil or Nothing

Despite all the modern aids provided by science, drilling for oil is still a gamble. Even with likely sites, the chances are less than 10% that oil will actually be found there. And even when oil is present, the chances are only 2% that it will be in commercially useful quantities.

..... The inventor who took the world's first photograph, in 1825, didn't dare ask anyone to pose for the shot. He photographed a building instead, which is hardly surprising, when you think that the exposure time was eight hours! ....

Downside-up

The following instruction is alleged to have originated from the Admiralty in London:

'It is necessary for technical reasons that these warheads should be stored upside-down. That is, with the top at the bottom and the bottom at the top. In order that there may be no doubt as to which is the bottom and which is the top, for storage purposes, it will be seen that the bottom of each warhead has been labelled with the word, 'TOP'.

Get to Work on That!

A fond grandfather in America sent for a hobby horse by mail order as a Christmas present for his granddaughter. The toy arrived packed in a large box, and it contained 189 pieces. The instructions stated that it could be put together in one hour.

Eventually, and just in time for Christmas, granddad managed to fit the bits together. When the time came to pay for the toy, he wrote a cheque, tore it into 189 pieces, and mailed it to the company.

Holding Your Breath for a Living

One way of earning a living in Ancient Greece was by salvaging valuable cargo from sunken ships. The going rate of pay was a tenth of the value of the goods in one metre of water, a third in four metres, and a half in eight metres.

Deeper than that? Without modern equipment, the diver didn't need to worry about getting paid – there was no chance that he'd survive at all.

Look, No Wheels

The Indians in America never invented the wheel, and didn't even see one until it was introduced with the arrival of the white man.

Their failure to reach this level of technology may be blamed on the fact that they had no horses or oxen, so they had few aids to carrying heavy loads. Sometimes they used dogs to pull a wooden frame along the ground, with the load placed on the frame.

To make up for this, though, the Indians were experts at making light bark canoes. As they travelled by water whenever they could, these craft ensured that they were just as mobile as their white invaders.

Kick Start

The human male has always had a weakness for measuring his strength. William Carter was trying to cash in on this when he invented the kick power meter in 1910.

For a small charge you could take a mighty swing at a dummy of a policeman. (Carter must have reckoned that the nature of the dummy acted as an incentive.) When your foot contacted the dummy's bottom, the head shot out on the end of an expanding neck. The neck was marked off with a scale, and this was the measure of your kick power.

WELL DONE, LADS. DID HE PUT UP MUCH OF A FIGHT?

Walkies?

If you get fed-up exercising your dog in all weathers, then it's a pity an invention of 1870 didn't catch on.

This was a vehicle with a large drum like a treadmill at the front. The driver sat behind on a comfortable seat, and steered with a wheel that controlled the direction of the drum. Dogs were placed inside the drum, and their job was to keep running, thus moving the drum forward.

Saddle Sore

Elijah Burgoyne thought that pedalling a bicycle was too much like hard work. So he invented a power unit known as the saddle pump.

The pump was fitted beneath the saddle and compressed air from the pump was fed into a cylinder under the crossbar. This was supposed to drive the turbine engine which turned the wheels of the bicycle.

And what worked the pump? Simple! The rider had to keep bouncing up and down on the saddle.

Spade Work

In 1921, William de Camp invented a counting spade. On the handle was a meter that recorded each dig.

What never became clear was why anyone would want to record the number of digs made. Perhaps the inventor had in mind the gardener who wished to prove something on a Saturday afternoon, but, not surprisingly, the device never became really popular.

. . . . . Bertha Delugi invented a nappy for caged birds . . . .

Don't Forget to Bend Your Knees

Benjamin Oppenheimer worried about what happened to people trapped by fire in skyscrapers. Evidently he was not impressed by the joke about the man who fell from the 60th storey and shouted, 'All right so far!' as he hurtled past the 30th.

So he invented an apparatus to deal with the situation. This was a parachute attached to a cap, which was strapped to the wearer's head. To absorb the impact of landing, the escaper was equipped with special shoes with thick soles and heels made of rubber.

Fortunately, the equipment was never used.

You Scratch My Back . . .

Does your dog spend all day trying to scratch those patches that he can't quite reach? The cure may lie in an invention of the early '70s.

This was an automatic animal scratcher, consisting of an electric-powered scratching arm mounted on a platform. First, the dog would have to be trained to step on to the platform, which would then switch on the motor and make the arm move up and down. Then, all the dog had to do was press the itching part of his body up against the end of the arm. Bliss!

However, the invention was not a success. Probably because most dogs are rather conservative creatures, and prefer to rub up against trees or fences.

. . . . . *Almost 60% of the resources of this planet are consumed by only 6% of the world's population: the people of the United States* . . . .

What Would Daisy Have Said?

The flying tandem would have been just the vehicle for honeymooners wanting to get away from it all – if it had worked.

It was the brainchild of an inventor named Gaunt. The 'aircraft' was made of an ordinary tandem with a pair of wings, a mast, and a large kite. Take-off would have been achieved by pedal power. Once airborne the riders would have turned two large propellers above them. But in the – likely – event of the propellers not providing enough lift, Gaunt thoughtfully included wings that flapped like those of a bird. These were also powered from the pedals.

The flying tandem never left the ground.

Whose Turn for the Rocker?

Many strange attempts were made to replace the ordinary sweeping brush before the coming of the electric vacuum cleaner. One such was the chair pump cleaner.

The cleaner required the labour of two people. One pushed the cleaner along, while the other sat and worked a rocking chair. The cleaner was joined by a flexible pipe to a bellows, which was operated by the rocking action of the chair. The bellows created a suction that picked up dirt and dust, and deposited it in the bellows. This was emptied later.

The big snag was that the rocking chair had to be carried from room to room – including upstairs!

A Zippy Idea!

It was a lady who invented a device to help zip up that awkward area between the small of the back and the base of the neck.

The equipment was attached to a wall. To dress or undress, the lady would have to back up to the invention and – somehow – hook the slide of her zipper over a catch fitted to the apparatus. This could then be moved up or down, as appropriate. The idea never caught on.

All for the Want of a Minus

The omission of one minus sign on a computer programme cost the US taxpayer more than $18 million.

It happened in 1962, when space probe Mariner I was being launched to take a close look at Venus. The lack of the minus sign made Mariner veer off course as the spacecraft separated from the booster rocket. NASA officials had to press a button to destroy both rocket and spacecraft.

Dam All Benefits

During the rainy season the Aswan High Dam in Egypt holds back the rising waters of the River Nile, which for thousands of years flooded farmland along the banks. Water collected by the dam was used to irrigate farmland during dry periods, and to generate electrical power.

But now the farmland which used to be fertilized by the silt in the floodwaters has to be enriched by expensive artificial fertilizers instead. And to produce these, the government has built fertilizer plants – powered by the electricity provided by the dam. In other words – they are almost back where they started.

A Cover-up Tail

In the days when transport was dominated by the horse, the state of the roads in cities was, to say the least, a mess – especially in wet weather.

One invention designed to clear things up was called the 'portable horse-bin'. This open-topped bag was suspended from the tail-strap of the horse's harness. Inside the bag was a little box full of disinfectant, which was opened automatically by the weight of the dung falling into the bag. The inventor pointed out that this was included 'in order to prevent any ill effects to drivers'.

He also suggested that bin boys should be employed at each cab stand and at the termini of omnibus and tram routes. The task of these lads was to empty the horse-bins into a larger bin in the middle of the road.

Give him his due, the inventor did see one objection to the widespread adoption of his invention. He admitted that many of the horses' tails were too short to hide the horse-bin to any great extent. But he suggested that this slight snag could be overcome by allowing the tails to grow longer.

WELL...WHAT D'YOU THINK OF STEPHENSON'S ROCKET LAUNCHED CUCUMBER?

Cool and Straight

In 1986 Chesterfield Council in Yorkshire bought a cucumber straightener for the local museum.

The straightener is, quite simply, a transparent glass tube open at one end. When a cucumber reached a certain size, it was placed in the tube, and continued to grow – straight. The device was invented by George Stephenson, the founder of railways in Britain, and the builder of the famous locomotive, *The Rocket*, in 1829.

Giving Up Arithmetic

The first personal computers to be made available to the public were the digital watch and the pocket calculator – in the late 1960s. Both had been made possible by research for the space programme.

In those early days the price of a pocket calculator didn't make it just the thing to help Johnny with his homework. It cost hundreds of pounds. But, unlike most things, the price has come down and down. By 1971 you could have one for £150. A year later it was £50. Now . . . well, most people can get one to satisfy their needs for less than £10.

Going for a Song?

One of the greatest technological boobs of all time was the original design for the famous Sydney Opera House. It was so way out that it had to be completely redesigned, giving Sydney the smallest opera house in the world.

Not only that, but the original budget of 7 million Australian dollars soared to 102 million. And still there wasn't room for a proper car park.

Bring on the Bridgesweepers

Four new minesweepers were built and ready in 1983 for the Italian Navy. All the latest technology had been incorporated, including glass-fibre hulls to prevent mines sticking to the vessels.

The manufacturers, Intermarine, had their shipyard a mile from the Mediterranean on the River Magra. All that remained was to launch the ships and sail them down to the sea.

Too late it was realized that there was a problem. The ships were too big to pass under a bridge at the head of the river. . .

What the Tramlines Left Behind

A dark, foggy night in 1933. Percy Shaw was driving to his home in Halifax, Yorkshire. Percy leaned forward, peering into the murk to take his bearings from the side of the road.

At last he reached the edge of the town – and the tramlines. There was a slight reflection from the shiny track. Percy breathed a sigh of relief and leaned back. That reflection made it possible to keep his car in a safe position on the road. What a pity there were no tramlines on the country roads!

It was then that Percy Shaw had the idea that made him a millionaire. Why not reflecting studs on the roads – like cat's-eyes? In 1936 the Ministry of Transport set up an experiment. Ten kinds of studs from different countries were put down on a busy road. After two years Percy's cat's-eyes were the only ones still in perfect condition and now millions of them are made every year for all parts of the world.

..... *Some computers use a laser beam to read information from a laser disc. Each disc can hold about 80 million words (about the number of words in 1,500 novels)* ....

Foot and Mouth

In the days before trains were heated, passengers could emerge from a long journey feeling frozen stiff, despite muffs, furs and hipflasks. But where there's a need, there's bound to be an inventor.

One came up with the idea that something should be done with all the warm air being breathed out by the people in the compartment. So the invention consisted of a cup which was secured over the mouth, with two tubes running down and attached, one to each foot.

Thus the passenger would breathe in cold air through the nose, breath warm air out through the mouth, and this would go straight down to the feet. No waste!

Ready for the Ambulance

In 1932, Heinrich Karl invented a device intended to make being knocked down by a car a less hazardous experience. He mounted a folded blanket on a collapsible frame and placed it above the car radiator. If the car hit a pedestrian, the frame would unfold and spread the blanket beneath the stricken patient.

Mr Karl's theory was that the pedestrian would fall into the blanket, thus being protected from landing heavily on the road. Alas, the inventor failed to find volunteers for field trials.

..... *Coding experts at the Pentagon in Washington are scratching their heads about what to do next. Their most complicated codes have been cracked by seven teenagers using ordinary computers* ....

Going Up

When the Sears Tower in Chicago was 'topped-off' in May 1974, it became the tallest building in the world. Although it and the World Trade Center both have 110 storeys, the Sears Tower at 1,454 feet is 104 feet higher than its rival.

A Hair-raising Tale

Barbers who didn't want to join the ranks of the unemployed may be to blame for the failure of an automatic electric barber invented in 1951.

It was a mask that fitted over the head, but left the face free. When the machine was switched on, exhaust jets on the outside of the mask pulled up the hairs on the wearer's head. With the hairs positioned for action, the cutting took place. But it wasn't cutting as we know it – it was singeing.

Inside the mask were electric elements, and these singed the hairs to the desired length. There were to be different masks for different styles of haircuts, and the whole operation was meant to be completed in a matter of seconds.

Damp Squib

A firework designed to be the most spectacular on record was engineered by George Plumpton of New York in 1975. It weighed 720 pounds, was forty inches long, and was designed to reach a height of 3,000 feet.

Crowds watched in hushed expectation as the inventor himself set the trail. As Mr Plumpton stood back, the firework hissed a little, then whistled for a bit, and finally blasted a ten-foot crater in the earth.

A Matter of Punctuality

In 1976 Bill Hancock lodged a complaint with a bus company in Staffordshire that ran a route from Hanley to Bagnall. He was annoyed because buses on the outward journey failed to stop, even when up to thirty people were waiting in a queue.

Councillor Arthur Cholerton responded to the complaint. His defence was that if the buses stopped to pick up passengers, the time-table would be disrupted!

Half Measure

The house journal of the Semi-conductor Equipment Materials Institute – trade association of the U.S. microchip equipment industry – is entitled, with touching candour, 'Semi News'.

Computer on the Rampage

The behaviour of a computer installed by Avon County Council in 1975 almost led to a search for clerks with quill pens.

The computer began by raising a school caretaker's pay from 75p to £75 an hour. Having been found out, it sulked for a while, and didn't pay a canteen worker at all for seven weeks. Then, just to show it really was on the side of the workers, it began dishing out £2,600 a week to a janitor. This honest soul sent the cheque back, but the computer was reluctant to admit its error. So, by return of post, it sent him another cheque for the same amount.

This must have given the computer confidence, for it then paid a deputy headmistress her annual salary each month, and gave assistants more salary than their department heads.

Finally, almost 300 council employees attended a protest meeting. When they found that only eight of them had been paid the correct salary, they all went on strike.

Guarded Comments

Early morning commuters in a train pulling into Liverpool Street station in London were disconcerted to hear the guard apologize over the public address system that 'for technical reasons' the train had arrived three minutes early.

Another early arrival, this time at Waterloo, caused the guard to announce, 'Those ticket holders who feel they have not had their money's worth from British Rail are perfectly welcome to stay on in their carriages for the extra five minutes if they want to.'

. . . . . A new company named Future Technology Ltd warned in its advertisements that the company's telephones were out of order. . . . .

Flying Imperial

Moves to bring down European air fares to something below piratical levels strike a chord in the 1926 Imperial Airways brochure of services between Croydon Aerodrome and the continent.

The return fare between London and Paris was £11.11 shillings that season – including a cabin trunk of luggage. And how reassuring the airlines were in those pioneer days.

'All pilots have brilliant records and long flying experience' and 'Each machine carries a highly trained and certified mechanic.'

Passenger comfort was given high priority. 'The passenger cabin is totally enclosed but well ventilated. And windows can be opened . . . ' 'Luncheon baskets can be provided on embarkation if ordered.'

Bank Note

Staff at the London branch of the Mitsui Bank have apparently not been as attuned as they should have been to Japanese working habits. They have been reminded in a memo from the management that though they can read magazines and newspapers during the lunch hour, 'after lunch hour you have to begin with your job.'

Food, drink, and personal phone calls, it is suggested, should not then be allowed to distract anyone from the job in hand. And the memo adds plaintively: 'Please don't sing a song during working hours.'

Unanimous

The legal profession prides itself on its ability to wrap a cutting insult within unexceptional language. But this exchange between a dissatisfied Englishman and a Scottish law firm is hard to beat.

'If this is an example of Scottish law,' wrote the outraged Englishman, 'thank God I'm not a Scotsman.' The law firm replied: 'Messrs . . . acknowledge Mr . . . 's letter and join with him in thanking God he is not a Scotsman.'

Legs, Legs, Legs

Scientists would dearly like to make a robot that could walk on two legs. Wheels are all very well on a smooth surface, and on some rough ground caterpillar tracks help. But as nature knows, there's nothing quite like legs for . . . well, climbing Mount Everest, for example.

Of course, it would be easier with four legs. But even then the robot could only move one leg at a time, which would be a very slow business, and not how four-legged animals move.

The US army tried to develop a four-legged truck for getting across very rough ground. The driver controlled it by movements of his legs and arms, which were linked to the four legs of the vehicle. The truck was so slow that it would have been a sitting target for enemy artillery and rockets, and the rocking motion made the driver seasick.

For Amusement Only

The first known steam engine was made more than 2,000 years ago in Alexandria, Egypt. The inventor was a scientist called Hero.

The engine was a hollow globe mounted on a pipe which ran to a kettle where water was boiled. Two L-shaped pipes were secured to opposite sides of the globe. The steam rushed out of the L-shaped pipes, causing the globe to whirl round.

The invention was looked on as an amusing toy and it occurred to no one that steam might be made to do useful work. Anyway, with plenty of cheap slaves available, why bother with engines? So the whole idea was forgotten, and 1,500 years passed before the first useful steam engine was developed in the 1600s.

Whoops!

... or accidents will happen ...

Banking Figures

The latest annual report for the old-established banking firm of Grindlays caused a few city heads to turn – it contained a centre-spread of glamorous girls in, and not quite in, tight tee-shirts.

But this wasn't meant to be coverage of a growth industry for the company – instead it was what turned out to be a popular printing error. Some waste pages were temporarily stapled into copies of the report during printing to prevent smears from drying ink. All these should have been removed, but a few copies were overlooked. And the fates that govern this banana-skin type of situation ordained that the waste pages should be leaflets of an eye-catching nature for a tee-shirt maker.

So now we know what city gents read behind those pink pages of the *Financial Times*.

Mayday, Mayday

The lifeboat was called out to a yacht in trouble in dirty weather. The coastguard, trying to get the yacht's exact location, called it on the radio. 'What is your position? Repeat, what is your position?'

And the answer came, faint but determined, from the skipper: 'My position . . . well, I'm the marketing director of a medium-sized computer software firm in the East Midlands.'

When Upstairs Came Downstairs

Free TV advertising to an audience of millions was the happy prospect for a demolition company contracted to blow up a tower block in Hackney, London. So 'L.E. JONES' was painted in bold letters all over the doomed building.

The cameras rolled, the charges exploded, and all seemed to be going well for Mr Jones. But, when the dust cleared, the upper half of the block was still there – balanced, intact and almost vertical.

Rasher Than Need Be

A man was driving his friend along a country road when a car suddenly appeared round a corner, and on the wrong side of the road. Both drivers swerved and a collision was avoided. But the woman who was driving the car lowered the window and shouted, 'Pigs!'

Amazed by this unprovoked abuse, the man muttered, 'Women drivers,' turned the corner . . . and drove straight into a herd of pigs.

Audible Early Warning

Some aviation accident investigators think that the time to start worrying during a flight is when the pilot starts whistling. An air transportation consultant in the United States has said that of more than 260 cockpit voice-recorded tapes removed from aircraft involved in accidents, ranging from the minor to the catastrophic since 1966, over 80% have a recording of the pilot whistling during the last half-hour of the flight.

Out of the Mouths . . .

A high-sided lorry tried to go under a railway bridge that was just a few inches too low. There was a grinding crash, and the lorry was wedged firmly between the road and iron girders.

Tugging and hauling were to no avail. The suggestion that an acetylene torch should be used on the girders of the bridge brought howls of protest from railway officials. There was talk of dismantling the lorry, but this was vetoed by the driver.

Then a small boy, who had been watching with interest, approached one of the worried officials. 'Hey, Mister,' he said, 'why don't you let the tyres down?'

A few minutes later the lorry was on its way.

A Lot of Bottle

Her husband had gone off to work, so the young wife decided to have a leisurely bath. She undressed and then remembered that the gas was still burning in the kitchen. Wrapped in a towel, she tripped downstairs. She was about to switch off the gas when she heard footsteps. The milkman! The arrangement was that he brought it into the kitchen to save the cream from the tits.

So she dashed to the nearest door – the broom cupboard – making it just in time. The footsteps grew louder. The cupboard door was flung open. It was the man from the gas company, come to read the meter.

For a moment she was speechless. Then she said, 'Sorry. I was expecting the milkman.'

It Came Away In My Hand

When James Callaghan was Prime Minister, he was invited to open the new premises of the Anglo-Austrian Society. A plaque was to be unveiled to commemorate the occasion.

Evidently, Mr Callaghan didn't know his own strength. When he pulled the cord, the plaque was torn off the wall.

A New Way of Losing an Audience

Professors are often thought to talk to themselves, but this Swedish lecturer in a university in California found it a particularly disconcerting experience. It all began well enough in a fully automated lecture hall with a packed audience. The splendid desk in front of the speaker included an array of buttons. He had been shown how to use some of them to dim the lights, draw the blinds, change the slides, and so on.

Warming to his subject, he leaned forward – placing both forearms firmly on the row of buttons. With a grinding noise, the audience sank out of sight. At the same time a dance floor closed over their heads. Within seconds, the lecturer was quite alone . . .

The Major's Orderly Withdrawal

A tombstone inscription:

Sacred to the memory of
MAJOR JAMES BRUSH
who was killed by
the
accidental discharge
of a pistol by
his orderly
14th April 1831
'Well done thou good and
faithful servant'

From the Jaws of Victory

So appalling was the military defeat of troops led by General Burnside in the American Civil War, that President Lincoln said of him: 'Only he could wring spectacular defeat out of the jaws of victory.'

The general had ordered his troops to cross a river by a very narrow bridge. There was so little space that the soldiers moved slowly and two abreast. They became a sitting target for the enemy, and were all shot.

Had the general explored other possibilities, he would have found that the river was only two feet deep. The troops could easily have crossed almost unseen.

..... A Russian interpreter translated 'Out of sight, out of mind' into Russian, and then back again into English. It came out as 'invisible lunatic' . . . .

Timber!

A police sergeant called to the scene of an accident found a car driven off the road into a wood. The driver was an RAF officer, obviously much the worse for drink.

Despite this, the officer said to the sergeant, with an air of authority, 'Shift the tree out of the way, so that I can press on.'

Stair-climbing Cow Floods Shop

In Inverness in 1954, some cows were waiting to be auctioned in a street where there were some shops. One of them broke out of the pen by way of an open gate. It ran into one of the shops and climbed a flight of stairs.

The floor above the shop gave way under the cow's weight. In trying to free itself from the debris, the animal turned on a tap and flooded the shop.

Reds Under the Chandeliers

A Dutch Foreign Minister was visiting Moscow for the first time. He had received a stern briefing about the possibility of electronic bugging in his hotel.

On arrival he set about a thorough examination of the room, scanning the walls, ceiling and floor for wires or tiny microphones. He was about to give up when he noticed a slight bulge in the carpet, leading from the wall to the centre of the room.

Lifting the carpet, he found a wire. With the cutters provided by his Intelligence Service, he snipped the wire. As he rose from his knees, there was a deafening crash from the room below as the chandelier fell from the ceiling.

Steady on the Pedals

The driver of a very old Mini was stopped by a policeman, who found that the car was not insured. The owner's excuse was that, having broken a leg jacking up the car, he had to drive it to get himself to hospital . . .

Toothless Pool Potter

Ken Richardson of Hemel Hempstead was enjoying his 32nd birthday celebration at the Oddfellows Arms. He played a game of pool and was about to make an easy pot when, unfortunately, his dentures fell out on the table. He potted them instead.

Ken's wife, seeing her husband's embarrassment, dashed to the pocket to bring the wayward teeth back into play. But it was not to be, for her hand jammed in the pocket, and stubbornly refused to emerge. Finally, firemen had to be summoned to get things back to normal with a power saw and washing-up liquid.

'Whoops!' Can Happen to Anyone

The Royal Society for the Prevention of Accidents was holding an exhibition. Special shelves were erected to display some of the exhibits. As people were walking round the display, the shelves collapsed, and one of the visitors was injured.

Vain Search for Peace

A 78-year-old grandmother living in Belfast felt that she wanted to spend the remaining years of her life away from the hate and violence. In 1970 she emigrated to New Zealand.

Two years later she was inadvertently caught up in an Irish civil rights march. She received a blow from a placard carried by one of the demonstrators, and died from head injuries.

What a sucker

Alfred Zuhl, aged 11, can claim the distinction of being sucked up whole by a vacuum cleaner. The lad was riding his bike when he skidded and fell in the path of a large street cleaner. Both Alfred and his bike vanished into the works.

The voracious machine was hastily dismantled, and Alfred emerged with little more than a few bruises.

Just Loosening Up!

Graham Smith, goalkeeper for Colchester, always carried out a pre-match routine. He kicked the base of one post, then ran across the goalmouth and kicked the base of the other. One Saturday it all went wrong when the crossbar descended with a crunch on his head.

But What Happened to the Burglar?

Soon after moving into a new house in Johannesburg, South Africa, the owner was awakened by the burglar alarm. He leaped out of bed, grabbed his revolver – and, the house being strange to him, walked through the glass partition between lounge and drawing-room. Suffering from cuts, he was taken to hospital.

Meanwhile, his wife set about cleaning up the mess. Water wouldn't shift the bloodstains, so she used petrol. On completing the job, she put the petrol into the lavatory, but forgot to pull the flush.

Then her bandaged husband returned. He relaxed on the lavatory, and lit a cigar. This mistake resulted in an explosion that threw him across the bathroom. The ambulance was again summoned, and he was carted off – this time on a stretcher.

To round off the night nicely, the ambulance men lost their way in the darkness of the garden. They stumbled over the rockery, tipping their patient on to the rocks. Added to his other injuries was a broken collarbone.

. . . . . 'I'm glad I'm not Brezhnev. Being the Russian leader in the Kremlin, you never know if someone tape-records what you say.' *Richard Nixon . . . .*

A Waste of Good Priming Time

Crooks in a factory at Vang in Norway were working with quiet, well-planned efficiency. They found the company safe and set a small explosive charge, just large enough to blow off the door. Having set the fuse, they retreated to the safety of the next room and waited confidently.

When it came, the explosion was shattering. The entire factory descended on the unfortunate heads of the crouching criminals. The trouble was that the safe hadn't contained what they thought – it was packed with dynamite!

Natural Gas

When John Stratton's wife left him, he was so distraught that he decided to put an end to it all. So he placed his head in the gas oven and breathed deeply. But John had not taken into account that the oven had been converted to natural gas, which is non-toxic. By the time he had given up trying, a feeling of relief and gratitude to the gas board had swept over him.

He decided to relax and think things over. As he did so he also lit a cigarette. Alas, this wasn't the best thing to do. John Stratton and the house were blown sky high.

Sharp Practice

The fastest goal recorded in a soccer match was scored by Brazilian international Roberto Rivelino, representing his club side Corinthians against Rio Preto at the Bahia Stadium.

Receiving the ball directly from the kick-off, Rivelino launched a left-footed drive towards the goal. The opposition goalie, Isadore Irandir, who had yet to conclude his pre-match prayers, was unable to get off his knees in time to save the ball.

Before the match could be restarted, Irandir's brother rushed on to the pitch, pulled out a revolver and delivered six shots into the ball. The crowd cheered as he was led away.

Sadie Comes Back for More

Mrs Sadie Tuckey of Ontario was knocked off her bicycle by a bus and killed. As the coffin was being carried, the mourners were shaken to see the 'corpse' suddenly sit up and scream. Sadie was far from dead. She leapt out of the coffin, dashed off down the road – straight in front of a bus. She was killed outright.

It Works, Baby!

A policeman in New York was worried about his girlfriend being mugged or even raped. So he bought her a spray of knock-out gas, and looked forward to giving it to her that evening.

He had a good clean-up after duty, had a bath and reached for his can of deodorant. Next thing he knew was waking up in hospital the following morning. He had sprayed himself with knock-out gas.

..... An undertaker in Twickenham put £1250 in a coffin for safekeeping. Alas, it was cremated by mistake ....

Return to Sender

A bank in Reno, Nevada, was the scene of a hold-up that went badly wrong in 1983.

The crook walked casually up to a cashier and handed her a note. It instructed her to put all the money into a bag and hand it over. The frightened girl obeyed, and the crook made his escape through the crowded city streets.

But there was a nasty shock for him when he reached home. The police were waiting to pick him – and his loot – up. The note he had given to the cashier had been written on the back of an envelope. On the other side was his address!

..... A strongman in Gloucester wanted to impress his friends after an evening at the local pub, so he went outside and lifted up the nearest car. Inside were two policemen, who arrested him...

Fingerlickin' Good

Austrian Airlines tell us in a flight brochure: 'Our most demanding passengers have discovered that a top chef has a finger in our delicious menus.'

Bumps in the Night

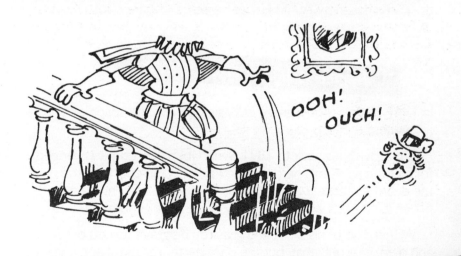

OOH! OUCH!

. . . or ghosties and ghoulies and long-legged beasties . . .

Aunt Harriet Rules

A real Scottish castle rebuilt in the Mohawk Valley, New York State, is the abode of a ghost known as Aunt Harriet.

In life, Harriet Cruger was a woman with a mighty strong will. It was she, with her love of all things Scottish, who ordered the building of the castle, and she ruled her domain with an iron fist. Once, when she got annoyed with her husband, she had their double bed sawn in half.

In death, Aunt Harriet continues to rule the roost. If things are not done in the castle in the way Harriet would have liked, the living are informed in no uncertain manner. Pictures swing, doors bang and cups are smashed to the floor. Though these are never the cups chosen by Aunt Harriet herself. . .

Protest from the Grave

In 1941, the grass on a grave in Wales grew in the shape of a cross . . . without the help of a living soul.

The story goes back to 1821, when John Newton was hanged for a crime he swore he did not commit. In the court, on the day the death sentence was passed, he called out, 'I am innocent and to prove it, no grass will grow on my grave for a generation.'

Within days of his burial the grass on his grave turned brown and died. Not only that, but the bare earth was the shape of a coffin.

Many attempts were made to break the curse of John Newton: the topsoil was removed and fresh earth laid on; grass seed was planted but the earth remained bare.

After more than fifty years, the beginnings of a slow change took place. Grass started to appear in patches, almost like filling in a jig-saw puzzle. But it took 55 years for the patches to come together . . . in the form of a cross.

Knot to be Expected

Most poltergeists just throw things about, but some are specialists – like this one in the home of Frances Smyth in Montreal, Canada.

Over a period of six weeks, almost everything that could be tied in a knot, was. That included clothes in the wardrobes, curtains at the windows, bed covers . . . One evening when the family returned home, they found that the arms of the overcoats of the five teenage boys had been done up in one huge complicated knot!

Extended Cover

'The most interesting 10 years of your life could start now,' promised Northern Rock Building Society in a circular addressed to 'R. M. de Berenguer, deceased,' and sent to the administrator of the estate.

Wash Out Your Mouth, Poltergeist

Many cases have been recorded of poltergeists using voices and speaking to the people they are tormenting. But almost always the voice used does not sound human. It is as if the poltergeist was having to master a new medium, the forming of sounds into words.

Very often the beginning of communication is just a series of grunts and moans. These gradually merge together, and become a gutteral voice. The words grow clearer as the poltergeist develops a sort of whisper.

The whisper progresses to a louder voice that is easy to understand – and then very often the bad language begins. Various researchers into the subject have used such words as 'foul', 'indecent', 'obscene' and 'disgusting' to describe the language used by poltergeists.

. . . . . In 99 per cent of poltergeist cases, there is present in the house a disturbed adolescent . . . .

'She Liked Ike'

General Dwight D. Eisenhower struck lucky when he was given a furnished apartment for life in a Scottish mansion, Culzean Castle in Turnberry. The living accommodation was a gift in appreciation for his leadership of the Allied Forces in World War Two.

His ghost was a dark-haired young woman dressed in an evening gown, who was not only beautiful, but also very polite. A Mrs Margaret Penney met her one day in a narrow corridor. Mrs Penney, who was plump, squeezed herself against the wall to allow the young lady to go by.

The gorgeous apparition paused, and then remarked 'I do not require any room nowadays,' and passed gracefully through Mrs Penney's side.

. . . . . Actress Olivia de Havilland once walked home from a party with a friend she hadn't seen for a long time. The next day she learned that he had died only hours before the party began . . . . . .

What Was Carlos Up To?

Top of the league of haunted houses in Britain was Borley Rectory, which stood near Sudbury in Suffolk. It was haunted on a grand scale from 1875 until the middle of this century, when it was gutted by fire.

An earlier owner, the Reverend Henry Bull, who had a family of seventeen children, had added a new wing to the building. Every one of the thirty-five rooms was haunted.

Almost every kind of ghostly carryings-on happened there – a girl in white, a nun, a headless man, and Henry Bull's dead son. Noises heard included the galloping of horses, dogs barking, bell-ringing, rushing water, smashing crockery, breaking windows, and a woman's voice that repeated loudly, 'Don't, Carlos, don't!' It was never learned whether Carlos did.

After Hours Apparitions

Do the spirits of dead drinkers return to their favourite pubs? That was the question in the mind of Elizabeth Harding when she took over the 500-year-old 'Swan Inn' in Essex.

The ghosts were a noisy lot: as the landlady lay anxiously in her bed after 'Time, gentlemen, please', she could hear ornaments crashing to the floor, the saloon doors banging and chairs being dragged around the bar. And her dog, used to a lifetime of bar-room life, refused to sleep downstairs.

It was not unusual for the lights to be blazing and the saloon doors blocked with chairs on the following morning.

I THINK YOU'VE RUPTURED YOURSELF

CHARITY PUSH OVER A PILE OF PENNIES

Unlucky Thirteen

Few people dared to spend a night, or an evening, at the old inn near Tisakurt in Hungary. Certainly local people stayed clear of the place, even during the day. But a few strangers, looking for a place to buy, had stayed there – though not for long! Always they left in terror, frightened away by the same ghastly apparition in the dining-room: thirteen phantom figures seated round the table, their lips curled back in the mirthless grin of death.

The old inn had been kept by Lazio Kronberg and his wife, Susi. There came a time when the couple had terrible problems. World War One had ruined their business, their daughter had run away to be a prostitute, and their son had left the house after being beaten by his father. The years ahead seemed hopeless. But they had a plan.

In the years 1919 to 1922, ten people ate their last meal in the old inn. The vintage wine after the meal was the killer – it was well-laced with strychnine. Each guest terminated his stay in a six-foot deep trench filled with quicklime in a nearby wood.

As the trench filled up, the wealth of the Kronbergs increased. The couple decided – just one more, and they would seal the trench for ever. The last guest was a jolly fat man, who carried a very heavy suitcase. It must contain something well worth while!

The meal was served, the vintage wine offered and sipped. The face of the jolly fat man convulsed as the others had done. He slumped in the remains of his meal. The Kronbergs searched the suitcase. There was a fortune in gold coins. But there was something else – a snapshot of the Kronbergs themselves! Horror dawned on the couple, and it gave way to a great grief. Their long-lost son had returned – returned with his fortune, and they had murdered him!

. . . . . A Scottish sportsman was once curious about his eight Kaffirs who were on a hunting expedition two hundred miles away; a Zulu witch doctor was able to tell him exactly what was happening to them . . . .

..... The voice of James Cagney's dead father once warned him to slow down when he was driving very fast. He did. Around the next corner was a car towing a caravan that had stalled in the middle of the road ....

Heart-stopper for a Heart-throb

People who are psychic are more likely to see ghosts than those who are not. Rudolph Valentino, heart-throb of the silent screen, was deeply psychic.

On his honeymoon in Europe, he took time off to see the ancient ruins of a castle. He was wandering through the gloomy dungeons and torture chambers when he had to stoop to enter a low doorway. Suddenly, he heard a scream of fear echo through the building.

About to beat a hasty retreat, he caught sight of large rusty hooks with chains dangling from the walls, and from one of the chains hung a skeleton, toes dangling just clear of the floor.

Intrigued, Valentino approached the skeleton and reached out to touch it. At that moment the terrible apparition disappeared.

There's a Corpse at the Door

A policeman's lot is not a happy one, especially, it seems, in Ghogte near Bombay. There, an unfortunate copper on duty outside a hospital mortuary opened the door one night only to be greeted by one of his charges – a 'corpse' with a slit throat.

The 'corpse' recovered nicely, but the astounded policeman went into deep shock ...

..... According to those who study psychic phenomena, Britain has the highest density of ghosts in the world ....

Your Turn, George

The ghost of Bessie Graves made sure that the man who made her a ghost got his just deserts. When living, Bessie had expected George Gaffney, who had made her pregnant, to marry her. But George had switched his affections to a more lucrative target, an elderly rich widow.

Then Bessie was found strangled with a silken cord embedded in the flesh of her neck. Scotland Yard detectives investigated, but there wasn't enough evidence to convict her lover.

Meanwhile, George was wooing in style. One evening he rolled up to the widow's house in a hansom cab. But as he neared his destination, he suddenly screamed. Sitting on the seat beside him was – Bessie! The ghost's eyes were glassy, and from the mouth lolled the swollen tongue.

A week later, George was entertained by the widow. During the evening she sent him to the cellar to fetch a bottle of wine, but George was only half-way down the steps when Bessie climbed out of the gloom. The silken cord swung from her neck, and the eyes stared even more glassily. George crashed headlong to the cellar floor.

After three weeks in hospital, George decided to leave England for Canada – widow or no widow – hoping to leave the shade of Bessie far behind him. Alas, on the evening before the journey he booked into a small hotel – and Bessie was there to greet him! The cord was no longer round her neck. It was in her hand, and she was holding it out to him.

George got the message. He sat down and wrote a full confession. Then he hanged himself.

. . . . . *Commander R. Jukes Hughes, serving in the Transkei, received a running commentary from local natives on a battle that was now taking place three hundred miles away – a commentary that proved to be accurate . . . .*

Sweet Dreams

Two stockbrokers were overheard drowning their sorrows in a City wine bar:

'All these changes in the share prices scare the life out of me,' said one. 'In fact, I worry so much, I either can't sleep, or have terrible nightmares.'

'I'm sleeping like a baby,' said the other. 'I wake every three hours and cry.'

Slay Ride

The headless ghost of Ormond Mallory rides its horse up the staircase of Castle Sheela in Ireland every Christmas night.

At the age of eighteen, Ormond was left a fortune by his father, and quickly began to squander it on every kind of indulgence. So disgusted was his mother with his behaviour that she returned to her native Hungary with the rest of her children – all daughters.

From then on, the domestic arrangements at the castle went to pieces. The only 'improvement' installed was a ramp by the main staircase, which allowed Ormond's dearly-loved horse to get to its master's bedroom, where it was allowed to sleep.

But one Yuletide, Ormond's mother returned, and arranged a huge party for Christmas night. During the day, Ormond went hunting, so the party was in full swing before he returned – in a most peculiar fashion.

The horse came to the castle door, and as it made for the ramp, the guests saw that tied to its back was the headless corpse of its owner – clearly grisly revenge for one of his worst misdeeds. The horse stumbled up the ramp, sank to the floor of the bedroom, and died.

Now, every Christmas night . . .

Phantom at the Opera

The old Metropolitan Opera House in America had a particularly unfriendly ghost. It was the wraith of former opera singer Mme Frances Alda.

Even in life, Mme Alda hated to see other singers being successful, and in death she did not change. Her ghost often rustled noisily into the audience, wriggled about in its seat, and crinkled its programme. When a soprano was on stage, it hissed, 'Flat! Flat!' and nudged its unfortunate neighbour. One opera-goer swears that her ribs were black and blue from the nudgings of the critical apparition.

Bloodstained Bandage Horror

Four men had been adrift in a dinghy in the Atlantic for 25 days, and they were crazed with hunger. Captain Rutt it was who made the suggestion that one of them would have to be eaten. Two of the shipwrecked sailors agreed, but 18-year-old Dick Tomlin said that he would never eat human flesh. So the obvious choice was to eat Dick.

The three survivors were picked up four days later. The captain of the rescue vessel was horrified to find Dick's remains under a tarpaulin. Back in England, the three were condemned to death for murder, but in view of the circumstances the Home Secretary commuted the sentences to six months.

After serving his time, one of the three, Josh Dudley, was employed as a drayman. Within a few weeks his team of horses saw something in the London fog that terrified them. They bolted, dashing Dudley to the road, where his skull was broken. Witnesses said that a figure swathed in bloodstained bandages appeared in the fog, and vanished after Dudley's death.

Badly shaken by this occurrence, Captain Rutt went looking for the third survivor, Will Hoon. He found the seaman, sodden with drink, in desperately bad health. Hoon was taken to the charity ward of a hospital. Within days he died screaming. Other patients in the ward said that a figure in bandages had held him down, and vanished when the seaman died.

Almost insane with terror, Rutt went to the police and begged to be locked up. In view of the man's mental state, they decided that it might be safer to put him in a cell for the night. That night at 3 a.m. screams of terror brought the police running to Rutt's locked cell. They unlocked the door and found Rutt on his bunk, his dead eyes staring. His hands were clenched, and locked in the fingers were shreds of bloodstained bandages!

Countdown

A five-year-old boy, Benjamin Blyth, was out walking with his father and asked him what time it was; his father said it was half-past seven. A few minutes later the child said: 'In that case, I have been alive . . . ' and named the exact number of seconds since his birth.

When they got home, his father took a sheet of paper and worked it out. 'You made a mistake – you were wrong by 172,800 seconds.' 'No I wasn't,' said the child, 'you forgot the two leap years in 1820 and 1824.'

Number Wonders

John and Michael are twins in a state mental hospital in America. Although they are mentally subnormal with an IQ of only 60, they can name the day of the week of any date in the past or future forty thousand years.

Asked, let us say, about 6 March 1877, they shout almost instantly: 'Tuesday.' And they have no more difficulty about a date long before the Great Pyramid was built.

Yet the twins have great difficulty with ordinary addition and subtraction and cannot even attempt multiplication and division.

From Beyond the Grave

A farmer named Michael Conley, of Ionia, Chicasaw County, was found dead in the outhouse of an old people's home, and his body was sent to the morgue in Dubuque, Iowa. Since the workclothes he was wearing were filthy, they were tossed outside the door of the morgue.

When the farmer's daughter was told that her father was dead, she fainted. And when she woke up, she insisted that her father had appeared to her and told her that he had sewed a roll of dollar bills in the lining of his grey shirt. She described precisely the clothes he was wearing – including slippers – and said that the money was wrapped in a piece of an old red dress that had belonged to herself.

No one took her dream seriously, assuming she was upset by her father's death. But the doctor advised them that it might set her mind at rest if they fetched the clothes. No one in the family had any idea of the clothes the farmer had been wearing at the time of his death. But the coroner confirmed that they were precisely as his daughter had described. And in the lining of the grey shirt, which still lay outside in the yard, they found a roll of money wrapped in a piece of red cloth and sewn into the bosom.

Home Grown

Daniel Dunglas Home was the most remarkable medium of the 19th century.

He performed his astonishing feats in broad daylight: he caused heavy articles of furniture to float up to the ceiling; he himself floated in at one window and out at another; he washed his face in blazing coals. He was tested dozens of times and never caught out in anything that looked like fraud.

And, in case you're thinking that someone as odd as this must have ended badly – he died at the age of 53, having spent his last years flitting between Russia and the French Riviera with his beautiful second wife. . .

The Sexy Spectre of Cannock

Some ghosts are, it seems, attracted by the 'emotional energy' of the living. Such was the case of the sexy ghost of Cannock in the Midlands. The ghost looked to be in his late thirties, and had black hair slicked back with some kind of astral hair dressing. It haunted the house of Denise Dyke and her mother, and had a way of leaping out of the wardrobe into the bed of the 17-year-old – when she was in it.

Even Ghosts Are Mortal

According to the experts, ghosts are not, as you might imagine, immortal. It seems that they begin to deteriorate after about 400 years. But there are exceptions to every rule, and one of these is a group of Roman soldiers that have been seen on three occasions marching in the cellars of the Treasurer's House of York Minster. Perhaps they are still looking for their back-pay!

The Grisly Hand of Tarrant Hinton

If you ever find yourself in the Dorset village of Tarrant Hinton, do not be worried if you see an unattached hand. The vision may have nothing to do with Hardy's Ale. The poor thing is simply looking for its arm.

It used to belong to Trumpet Major Blandford, a member of the dragoons, who did a little poaching on the side. He was surprised by gamekeepers in December 1880. There was an exchange of gunfire, during which Blandford's hand was severed. He escaped to London, but there he died. Villagers gave the hand a decent burial in the churchyard, but at times it does feel lonely...

Doctor! Doctor!

... or strong medicine ...

Cool-Aid

Researchers in Canada claim to have found a new way of easing toothache. It's a sort of do-it-yourself acupuncture – but without the needles. On the back of the hand is the 'Hoku' point, and it seems that rubbing ice on it works almost as well as needles.

So, in the small hours when it can be difficult to get hold of a dentist, visit the fridge instead!

No Respecter of Authority

When the plague known as the Black Death struck London in 1348, it was no respecter of persons. One of the first to flee the stricken city was the Abbot of Westminster. He was also one of the first to die.

In the space of one year, three successive Archbishops of Canterbury died.

New Teeth for New

So transplants are nothing new! Here is some advice from *The General Practice of Physic*, a publication of 1793:

'It is now become a Practice, especially in France, upon drawing a sound Tooth, to replace it in its Socket; where, with proper Precautions, it will fasten again. After the Extraction of the Tooth, have a Gargle of Honey, mixed with the Juice of the Herb Mercury, common Salt, and Spring-Water, and then put it in its former place; and it will become more useful than before.

'The French Operators have improved this Hint; and when the Tooth is rotten, or otherwise unfit to be replaced, they put another sound human Tooth in the Room of it, when it can be had; otherwise one of any other Animal, that is of a Size suitable for the purpose.'

But why draw a sound tooth in the first place? Odd!

Gardening with Tears

An eight-year-old boy in Cape Town, South Africa, was sent home from school one day with a swollen eye. The condition became worse, so his parents took him to a doctor. An examination showed a seed and sprout growing out of the left eye. It seems that his eyeball provided the essential conditions for germination: moisture, warmth, fresh air, and protection from strong light.

Microsurgery removed the growing plant from just under the surface of the eyeball, though it's likely the lad will never be keen on gardening.

Once Every Four Hours

Sufferers from arthritis who want a change from pain tablets might like to try an effective substitute . . . sex.

A director of the National Institute for Human Relationships in America says the sexual activity stimulates a release of additional cortisone into the blood, which reduces pain and swelling in inflamed joints. Arthritis patients were interviewed on the subject, and up to 70% of them confirmed that sex did help.

The soothing effect lasts from four to six hours. So the prescription is much the same as for pain tablets!

The Head of the Queue

The scene: a crowded doctor's waiting-room in Birmingham. There is an air of impatience.

Enter a Pakistani, who strides towards the surgery. A woman stands up, grabs him by the arm and says, slowly and deliberately, 'We are all before you. Do . . . you . . . understand?'

The Pakistani replies, equally slowly and deliberately, 'No, you are all after me. I . . . am . . . the . . . doctor.'

There's No Justice!

An inmate of Ohio State Penitentiary, Charles Justice, helped to design the jail's first electric chair. After his release, he committed a murder and was condemned to death. The place of execution was Ohio State Penitentiary. The instrument of execution was the electric chair.

Bandit on the Run

When the pop group Revolver were on holiday in Israel in 1969, their minibus was held up by a bandit. One of the group, Tony Price, found himself looking down the barrel of a sub-machine gun. 'Drive on,' said the bandit, 'or I'll blow your head off.'

Tony did drive on — fast — into a deep pile of sand. The bandit was flung forward and his gun went off, injuring his foot. Tony grabbed the gun and shoved the wounded crook out of the bus. The last they saw of him was a dejected figure, limping off into the dunes.

The police found him later, however, following his trail of blood.

..... *Advertisement in the British Medical Journal: 'Surgical instruments: complete assortment of deceased surgeons.'* ....

Pin Money

In days gone by the Chinese used to pay their acupuncturists only if they remained healthy. A farmer who became too ill to work despite treatment would expect his acupuncturist to do his work for him.

Ruling-class families often kept an acupuncturist in their homes, and a severe illness or death in the family could result in the unfortunate man being beheaded.

Courtroom Crack

Court usher Jan Pearce, aged 64, of Plymouth, soon regretted his offer to be PC Brian Stable's guinea pig.

As the PC prepared to demonstrate an arm-hold necessary to detain a prisoner, a loud crack echoed through the court-room. At first the policeman thought he had torn the usher's shirt; in fact Mr Pearce's arm was broken.

The Constable was one of his most devoted visitors in hospital.

..... *A hundred Spanish paratroopers had a special meal to celebrate an accident-free drop. Before they reached the coffee, they were all rushed off to hospital with food poisoning* ....

The Bump was a Drunk

Late one night in 1983, Mrs Sally Solomons was so fed up at having to wait for the return of her husband from a drinking session with the boys that she decided to go out and fetch him herself.

As she reversed the car by the front door, however, there was a nasty bump. Sally got out to look, and found she had driven over the prostrate form of her husband. Alas, he hadn't quite made it to the door!

Superman's Crash Landing

David Webb of Doncaster spent an evening watching videos of his hero, Superman. Later that night, in his dreams he *was* his hero, flying here and there on missions of mercy. But in the morning he woke up in the garden with broken ribs, a dislocated jaw and numerous bruises. It seems that he 'flew' out of the window in his sleep.

Knock-out Dinner

When the butler of the 19th century Scots physician James Simpson went into the dining room to clear away after a dinner party, he found all the guests stretched out across the table, fast asleep. But for once this wasn't because the conversation was exceptionally boring, or the food terrible. Instead, it was all in aid of an experiment.

Simpson was a pioneer in the use of chloroform as an anaesthetic, and after dinner he had asked his colleagues to take a whiff of the gas. They all agreed – and quickly found themselves falling asleep where they sat.

Despite this success, doctors were very slow to accept the idea of an anaesthetic for surgery. The person who really made the notion popular was Queen Victoria, who took chloroform to dull the pain of childbirth. And who can blame her – she had nine children in all!

Not Hear, Hear

A man in New York wore a hearing aid for almost 25 years despite a suspicion that it wasn't working as well as it ought. Then, during a visit to the local hospital, it was discovered that it had been fitted to the wrong ear. When it was switched over the man found he could hear normally again – for the first time in nearly a quarter of a century!

Stiff Task

American woman overheard in a Mayfair bar: 'Joe's not as limber as he used to be. These days, it's as much as he can do to touch his knees without bending his toes.'

Living by Numbers

Being ill at sea in an old sailing ship was a chancy business. The ships didn't carry a doctor, so the job was done by the ship's captain, who had no medical training.

But there was a system – of sorts! Each captain had a sea chest of medical remedies, and a copy of a manual entitled, *Cox's Companion to the Sea Medicine Chest*. This manual listed and numbered most of the known diseases, as well as their symptoms and remedies.

When a seaman was taken ill, the captain, with the manual handy, carried out a short inspection. He then boldly announced the disease and its number, and prescribed a remedy with the matching number.

Unfortunately, there were times when the supply of particular remedies ran out. At least one captain, when there was a shortage of remedy number 7, simply mixed the remedies for diseases 3 and 4, and used the result as a replacement.

... MEDICINE CHEST'S EMPTY SO WE'LL JUST HAVE TO SING DISEASE No. 676..

Letting off Steam

A doctor in 1837 who was, naturally, interested in the effects of drugs, gave a friend some hemp — more familiar to us as marijuana. Having taken the stuff, the guinea pig sprang from his seat, shrieked with laughter, and shouted, 'Oh, ye gods! I'm a locomotive!'

For about three hours the happy man paced to and fro with measured stride, breathing out in violent gasps. When he spoke, he divided his words into jerked syllables, at the same time using his arms like the cranks of imaginary wheels.

The climax arrived when he was about to quench his thirst with a cup of water. He suddenly put it down without drinking, and exclaimed, 'How can I fill my boiler when I'm letting off steam?'

Just the Bare Bones

Human bodies for dissection were eagerly sought during the 18th century. A prize to be regarded with reverence was the body of one O'Brien, an Irish giant of seven feet seven inches. A famous dissector named Hunter determined to have it at all costs. But O'Brien had heard of Hunter's intentions, so he took special precautions to avoid the dreaded scalpel.

Before he died, O'Brien persuaded several of his countrymen to take his body to the sea, and sink it in deep water. Hunter, meanwhile, was in cahoots with the undertaker, and arranged to have the coffin locked in a barn while the mourners rested at an inn during their long progress to the coast. Just as Hunter had hoped, the mourners drank deeply and slept soundly. The coffin was opened and the huge corpse extracted. Then stones were placed in the coffin, and the lid secured.

Triumphantly, Hunter transported the magnificent specimen back to his surgery in Earl's Court, where O'Brien was soon reduced to one of the longest skeletons in the business.

All Wrapped Up in His Work

Doctors were set an unusual problem when a van rolled up to a casualty department at Southend in August, 1978. In the back of the vehicle was Janos, the Incredible Rubber Man, and he needed help – badly!

It seems that he was lowered to the floor of the circus, hanging from a trapeze. His legs were wrapped up behind his head. This was quite normal. What wasn't normal was that he stayed that way, despite the best efforts of himself and all his friends. It took doctors half-an-hour to sort out Janos. They then ordered him to lie flat on his back for a week.

The Good Old Days

According to one school of medical opinion in the 19th century, plunging children into cold water cured them of convulsions, coughs, inflammation of the ears, navel and mouth, rickets, pimples and scabs, suppression of urine, vomiting and a want of sleep.

Bathing in cold water was also recommended for a wide range of adult afflictions. It was suggested that, 'In winter, snow may be mixed with the water. With weaklings, warm water may be used at the beginning, then by and by, colder, and lastly quite cold water.'

Yellow For Go

Depressed? Need cheering up? Well, American doctor Elior Kinarthy says you don't need pills or drugs. Just look at something yellow. He has dozens of patients who simply carry a yellow card in their wallet and gaze at it for ten seconds when they're feeling down.

Wonder what colour his bills are. . .

The Surly Bonds of Earth

Jacques Lefèvre left nothing to chance when he decided to commit suicide. He tied a noose round his neck and fixed the end of the rope to a stake at the top of a cliff. Jacques then drank some poison, set fire to his clothes, and hurled himself over the cliff. At the last moment, he even tried to shoot himself – just to make sure.

By chance, the bullet missed Jacques, but cut the rope. Free of the threat of hanging, he plunged into the sea. The sudden ducking extinguished the flames, and made him vomit the poison.

A well-intentioned fisherman picked him up, and took him to hospital, where he died – of exposure!

Who Put That There?

A Great Surgeon, in whose presence lesser mortals trembled, was engaged in some difficult bowel surgery. His houseman, new to the job and very nervous, was keeping the patient's liver out of the Great Man's field of action.

After some time the Great Surgeon realized that the patient's arteries were not pulsating as they should, and he informed the anaesthetist of the fact. The anaesthetist confirmed that the heart had indeed stopped beating.

Cool as a cucumber, the Great Surgeon cut through the diaphragm, and began massaging the heart from inside the patient's chest. The houseman, functioning as he should, dashed off to get the emergency drugs suitable for the occasion. He primed a syringe with adrenalin, and fitted a long needle specially designed to inject the drug straight into the heart. Without hesitation he plunged the needle through the skin, between the ribs – and straight into the Great Surgeon's hand!

Night Shadows

A doctor not long qualified was in charge when a young girl was brought into hospital with fairly severe asthma. The time was 3 a.m. When the X-rays arrived, he saw that at the top of each lung there were vertical shadows of an unusual shape. He studied them, but could make nothing of them. Becoming alarmed, he rang up the consultant and called him out from his bed.

When the consultant arrived, he looked at the X-rays and at the girl. Then he turned to the doctor. 'You fool!' he grated between bared teeth. 'These are her pigtails!'

. . . . . A man in Stroud swallowed a pint of periwinkles, complete with shells. On request, he repeated the feat, and died . . . .

Campbell's Patent Poison Extractor

John Bunyan Campbell believed that the true secret of health was to get poison out of the body before it did any damage.

He reckoned that the body battles against three kinds of poison: animal, vegetable and mineral.

So he invented an electrical poison extractor. Patients suffering from one of these afflictions had to sit on a chair with their feet bared. Positioned below the feet was a poison receiver, which contained an appropriate object, such as a piece of raw meat, a lump of iron, or a vegetable. A positive electrode was attached to the patient's neck, with a negative electrode on one of the feet.

When all was in place, the electricity was switched on, and a current flowed through the patient's body. The idea was that the current would collect the poison *en route*, and at the end of its journey deposit it safely in the receptacle. A course of treatment was 6-8 sessions of thirty minutes each.

No records of results have been left to posterity, and readers are not advised to experiment with the idea.

A Gathering of Talent

While walking in Hove, a doctor noticed a crowd of people gathered round a prostrate figure on the pavement, so he decided to offer his professional skills. Bending over the patient as he approached was a man in tweeds. The doctor announced his qualifications, and was about to brush the fellow aside, when the tweedy character protested loudly, saying, 'I am a fully qualified instructor in First Aid with the St John Abulance Brigade.'

An argument ensued, during which the patient lay neglected on the pavement. But the vacuum was filled by a lad of eighteen, who pushed forward, declaring that he was a second-year medical student. The lad had hardly got to work when a lovely blonde appeared, knelt by the supine figure, and applied an ear to the chest.

Then she looked up and became aware of a certain tension in the air. She smiled sweetly and said, 'Oh, it's quite all right, I'm a social worker!'

. . . . . A Scotsman in court who was answering to a charge of poaching, said, 'I shot the pheasant because it was looking ill.' . . . .

Cough or Car Medicine?

Doctors in the old days often prescribed the drinking of tar-water for coughs, bronchitis and asthma. Patients were advised to pour a gallon of cold water on to a quart of tar, stir well and let stand for two days. When the tar had settled on the bottom, the water was bottled. Half a pint of the concoction was taken morning and night, and patients were advised that it was less unpleasant to drink the stuff if the nostrils were held at the same time.

The tar itself could also be used for 'greasing of coach or cart wheels'.

. . . . . *'We are sorry to announce that Mr Albert Brown has been quite unwell, owing to his recent death, and is taking a short holiday to recover.' Note in Parish Magazine* . . . .

What Doctors Are For

Konrad Adenauer, who was German Chancellor, developed a bad cold when he was in his late eighties. A doctor was summoned. After examining the old man, the doctor said, 'Please don't expect miracles. I can't make you any younger, you know.'

Adenauer responded, 'I don't expect you to make me younger. The main thing is that you should succeed in making me older.'

Under the Spotlight

Spotlight

... or tales of the famous and infamous ...

Bailing Out the Great

Herbert Sutcliffe's fame is legendary in the world of cricket. He was at the height of his powers when he consented to play in a charity match between two village teams in Yorkshire. Instead of the usual few dozen spectators on the day, thousands turned up.

Pleased by his pulling power, Herbert decided to thrill the faithful following with a six off the first ball. So he stepped out of the crease and opened his shoulders, determined to thrash the ball over the pavilion.

But the turf was not as smooth as at Lord's. The ball bounced well above the flailing bat, and into the hands of the wicketkeeper. In a flash, he whipped off the bails and yelled, 'Howzat!'

For a second there was a breathless hush. Then the umpire roared, 'Not out!' A sigh of relief went round the vast crowd.

In a voice low but full of menace, the umpire said to the wicket-keeper, 'Tha great blithering blockhead! Dost think these folk hez cum to watch *thee* stump?'

..... The inventor of the modern lavatory system, Thomas Crapper, wrote an autobiography entitled 'Flushed With Pride' ....

Churchillian Modesty

A woman once said to Winston Churchill, 'Are you not thrilled to know, Mr Churchill, that every time you make a speech, the hall is packed to overflowing?'

The great man replied, 'Yes indeed, it is quite flattering. However, when I feel this way, I always try to remember that if, instead of making a speech, I was being hanged, the crowd would be twice as big.'

A Quick Starter

At four years of age, when most of us make 'music' by banging pan lids together, Wolfgang Amadeus Mozart was composing minuets and other pieces.

At the age of six he was playing before kings, and at seven he published violin and harpsichord sonatas. At eight he was performing the works of Bach and Handel before the English Court, and at ten writing his first oratorio. His first opera was written when he was fourteen.

Walking All Over Garbo

If you want to walk on the features of the great film actress, Greta Garbo, visit the National Gallery in London.

On the floor of the main centre landing of the entrance hall, her features are part of a mosaic representing the 'Awakening of the Muses'. The originals of the Muses are famous writers and other artists. Garbo lent her features to the Muse of Tragedy.

..... The Welsh poet Dylan Thomas set his famous radio play in verse, 'Under Milk Wood', in an imaginary Welsh village, Llareggub. The name spelt backwards means just that ....

Royal Death

Charlemagne, King of the Franks and Holy Roman Emperor, did not allow even death to interfere with his royal dignity. In the year 1,000 his tomb was opened in Aachen Cathedral in Germany. His remains were revealed, seated on a throne, a crown on his head — well, skull — a globe in one hand, a sceptre in the other, and the imperial mantle on his shoulders.

Bacon and Chicken

Francis Bacon, 16th century philosopher and statesman, would have lived longer if he hadn't branched out and tried an early experiment in refrigeration.

Snow lay on the ground when Bacon and a friend were riding along in a coach. Bacon wondered if snow might not preserve flesh, as salt was used to do in those days.

The pair bought a hen from a woman in a nearby cottage, killed it and stuffed it with snow. Unfortunately, the snow so chilled Bacon that he caught a cold and died three days later.

Dewhiskered Hyena

Julius Jacob von Haynan, an Austrian general in the 19th century, was known as 'the hyena of Brescia'. He was notorious for the savage cruelty with which he suppressed revolutionary movements in Italy and Hungary. During a visit to a London brewery, he was set on by infuriated workmen who tore out his whiskers.

Job for Life

After conducting a concert in 1939, Sir Thomas Beecham returned to his hotel. He saw a lady sitting in the foyer whose face he knew well, but for the life of him he could not attach a name to it. But he greeted her, and said, 'I do hope you enjoyed the concert.'

There followed some small talk, and then Sir Thomas remembered that the lady had a brother. He said, 'How is your dear brother, and what is he up to at the moment?'

The penny dropped when the lady replied, 'Oh, he's still King, you know.'

Photographic Memory

The English historian Thomas Macaulay could read a page of print once, and immediately repeat it from memory. It is said that he could memorize rapidly the entire contents of a book, and later repeat them almost without a mistake.

Hanging On to Dear Life

Rasputin, sometimes known as the Mad Monk of Russia, proved hard to kill. In 1916, a group of high noblemen decided that the holy man's influence on the Czar was doing nobody any good. So they decided to assassinate him.

Rasputin became the victim of a series of attacks, all in one day. He was stabbed, shot and poisoned, but all to no avail. Finally, the assassins successfully completed the job by throwing him into the ice-cold waters of a river.

In fact, it was all a waste of time, because the Russian Revolution broke out within three months.

It's the Thought that Counts

Ecuador is not a rich country, but it was felt that the Ecuadorian poet, José Olmedo, deserved a statue in his honour. Instead of commissioning a sculptor to do the job however, it was decided to make do with an unwanted statue of the English poet, Lord Byron.

Cashing In

A boy at boarding school was broke, so he wrote to his grandmother, politely requesting a small funding. The response was a lecture on the evils of extravagance – but no money.

A few days later Granny received another letter. It read: 'Dearest Grandmamma, I received your letter, and hope you will not think I was disappointed because you could not send me any money. It was very good of you to give me good advice. I sold your letter for four pounds ten.'

The schoolboy became King George V. 'Granny' was Queen Victoria.

We Should Have Brought the Cat

If you're feeling out of your depth in grand company, the golden rule is to do exactly what your host or hostess does. Or is it?

Guests of President of the United States Calvin Coolidge followed this advice at a formal White House dinner. All through the meal they kept an eye on his every move and followed just moments behind. Then, when the coffee arrived, the President startled his guests by pouring half of it into his saucer. Unsure of the procedure, they followed suit. Then he added cream and sugar. So did they.

But they were completely disconcerted when he leaned down and placed the saucer on the floor. After all, there was only one cat!

. . . . . As a way of warding off evil spirits, the legs of Disraeli's bed stood in bowls of salty water . . . .

The Second Coming

During a reception at Number 10, Downing Street, Mrs Mary Wilson was entertaining guests while her husband was completing some urgent paperwork upstairs. A group of the guests were discussing religion, and one of them said, 'At least we know there is one above who knows all the answers.'

Having heard only the last sentence of the discussion, Mrs Wilson said brightly, 'Yes, indeed. Harold will be down in a minute.'

Unsung Heroes

Sir Edmund Hillary and Sherpa Tensing will be for ever remembered as the men who first conquered Everest. What is often forgotten is that their triumph would have been impossible without the backing of twelve other expert climbers, 40 Sherpa guides and more than 700 porters.

Echo from the Past

When Humphrey Bogart, star of the film 'To Have and Have Not' was buried in 1957, a gold whistle was placed in the coffin with him.

The whistle was put there by his wife, Lauren Bacall, who appeared in the film with him. She had the whistle inscribed with this line from the film: 'If you need anything, just whistle.'

..... The original 'Nosey' Parker was Matthew Parker, Archbishop of Canterbury from 1559, who had an unenviable reputation for not minding his own business. He also had an extremely long nose ....

You Must Be Joking!

When two temperaments as different as General Eisenhower's and the actor, Michael Caine's, come into contact, sparks fly.

Michael Caine was doing his National Service in Germany, when his unit was visited by the General. Caine's platoon had been instructed to dig fox-holes, to give Eisenhower something to inspect.

While they waited for the arrival of the top brass, it rained heavily. For some hours Caine stood at the ready, up to his hips in water. When Eisenhower turned up at last, he asked Caine if he was thinking of staying in the army. The answer was a very positive, 'No thanks!'

Caine was confined to barracks for a month.

The Marriage of Heaven and Hell

The wife of the English poet William Blake used to complain that her husband spent so much time in heaven that he rarely spoke to her. According to Blake, he had long conversations with the bible prophets and other people famous in history.

With Spots On

The bandleader in a fashionable restaurant made the grave mistake of sending a note to the famous playwright, George Bernard Shaw, who was sitting at a table. The note asked Shaw if there was anything he would like the band to play.

Immediately the reply came back, 'Yes, dominoes.'

A Question of Parts

Lord Mountbatten once visited Malta to film scenes for a television series about his life. He was met at the airport by a young and rather over-eager reporter from the local radio station.

They talked about the series for a while, before the reporter asked seriously, 'And what part will you be playing in the series, Lord Mountbatten?'

But the Greatest of These is Charity

During a charity ball, George Bernard Shaw asked a dowager for a dance. The lady exclaimed, 'Oh, Mr Shaw, what made you ask poor little me to dance?'

To which Shaw replied, 'Well, this is a charity ball, isn't it?'

All Rounder

Most people think of the great W. G. Grace as one of the finest cricketers of all time. But few are aware of his prowess in a number of other sports. For example, during 1866, following a score of 224 not out over two days against Surrey, he went on to win the 440 yards hurdles at the National Olympian Association meeting at Crystal Palace.

Something To Be Grateful For

The famous author, Charles Lamb, was often mistaken for a clergyman, because of his habit of wearing a white cravat. Once at a dinner party he was asked to say grace. Lamb surveyed the company and said, 'Isn't there a clergyman present?'

When he was told there was not, he bowed his head and said, 'Let us thank the Lord.'

Giving Things a Lift

Derrick, the hangman, was so efficient at his job that, when he was condemned to death for a criminal offence, the Earl of Essex pardoned him. The sting in the tale for Essex was that when his turn came to be condemned to death for treason, it fell to Derrick to carry out the execution.

But Derrick's fame does not end there. So well known did he become during the fifty years of his grisly career, that the hangman's gibbet became known as a derrick. And then, when modern cranes were constructed, they were referred to as derricks, because of the similarity of the shapes.

In fact, the word *derrick* is now used for many devices involved in moving heavy weights, and even for the framework of an oil well.

. . . . . Denis Norden, the scriptwriter and broadcaster, once asked a lady at a party, 'What happened to that skinny blonde your husband used to be married to?' Came the reply, 'I dyed my hair.'. . . . .

On Your Knees!

Tourists to Britain are often overawed by the archaic customs of our great institutions.

One day a party was being shown round the House of Commons. Down one of the corridors they saw approaching the Lord Chancellor's procession, led by Lord Hailsham. As he passed the excited group, the famous peer caught sight of an old friend walking just behind them. He raised an arm and called out, 'Neil!'

The tourists dropped to their knees.

. . . . . When Hitler's Central Bank Governor was told that Hitler was dead, he said, 'I wouldn't believe Hitler was dead, even if he told me so himself.'. . . . .

What Service!

In the London Marathon of 9th May, 1982, Roger Bourban, a waiter from Beverly Hills, ran the full course in waiter's regalia. Not only that, but he carried a free-standing, open bottle of mineral water on a tray (weighing 3lb 2oz) all the way.

His time, which was 2hrs 47mins, was faster than those of the winners of the first four marathons of the modern Olympic Games.

Dead Wrong

Mayoral candidate Stanley Goldman, 69, died of a heart attack in Hollywood, minutes after a speech accusing his opponent of being too old for the job.

Death of a Legend

In 1860 an advertisement appeared in the *San Francisco Herald* which read:

'WANTED: Young, skinny, wiry fellows, not over eighteen, willing to risk death daily. Orphans preferred. Wages $25 per week. Apply Central Overland Pony Express.'

The cinema has made the Pony Express renowned throughout the world, but in fact it only lasted for 18 months and was a financial flop. The idea was to provide an express mail service from Missouri to California, by the fastest route – and that meant difficult country infested with hostile Indian tribesmen. Many of the young, skinny, wiry fellows ended their career with an arrow in the back.

The only people who used the service were those who needed to send urgent messages across the continent. But shortly after it had begun, the first telegraph wire across the country was completed. From then on, 'urgent' could mean 'instant'. It was the death of the Pony Express.

Jammed and Slammed

Renowned in the Royal Navy is the frigate HMS *Ulster*, which made the most remarkable manoeuvre in May 1966.

It was on training exercises in the Tamar estuary at Plymouth when the engine control jammed in the 'half astern' position. A frantic attempt to unjam it left it on 'full astern'. The ship picked up speed and sailed backwards towards a stone jetty.

The captain's attempt to telephone the engine-room having failed, he ordered an officer to go down and explain the situation. But the officer could make no headway down against the entire ship's company all heading up to emergency stations. When the frigate hit the jetty, the ship was instantly shortened by seven feet. This compressed the air inside the vessel to such an extent that a sailor was shot through a hatch and landed on the jetty – uninjured!

How's Your Banting?

If you are into slimming at the moment, then you are banting. It's not a word much used nowadays, but it's in the dictionary for all to see.

It goes back to a London cabinet-maker, William Banting, who was 66 years of age, short and very, very fat. He went on a diet, cutting out butter, sugar, milk, beer, soup, potatoes and beans. Banting ate only meat, fish and dry toast.

More than cold feet

Joanna the Mad really was crazy about her husband, Philip the Handsome of Spain. But perhaps she carried things a little too far when he died. Grief-stricken, Joanna refused to bury the corpse. Instead she kept it in her bed for over three years . . .

Cool Cuban

Fidel Castro of Cuba stands head and shoulders above other contenders for the honour of being the politician who has survived most assassination attempts. By 1984 he had notched up an estimated 24 not out.

He has been missed by poison pellets, shells exploded in Havana harbour and students wielding bazookas. Objects having failed so often, a beautiful blonde agent was sent in to try her luck. But she fell in love with her bearded target and so gave up her deadly mission.

..... Victor Hugo, the famous French author, found the discipline of writing each day very difficult. Sometimes he instructed his servants to steal his clothes in the morning, so that he could not go out ....

Auto Suggestion

Some noisy collisions between motoring buffs are soon to be expected. The wily French have started down what looks like being an accident-prone circuit, for their motor manufacturers have a plan to bolster national pride – and obtain some welcome international publicity for their marques – by proclaiming a Frenchman, Edouard Delamarre-Debouttevill, the true inventor of the motor car.

The French claim that this citizen of Rouen took to the road with a petrol-driven automobile in May 1883, and had his patent registered in 1884. While the Germans have not, so far, begun massing tanks on the Rhine to avenge what they see as a national insult, they have started a paper war to defend the name of their much-revered Gottlieb Daimler.

They assert that he, more than any other man, was responsible for the birth of the motor car through his development of lightweight, fast-running, internal combustion engines. Dr Bernd Gottschalk of Daimler-Benz, makers of Mercedes cars, says historians agree that the first functional automobile ran in 1886 and it was a joint production by Daimler and Karl Benz – co-founders of Daimler-Benz.

Lord Montagu, who runs the national motor museum at Beaulieu, has weighed in saying that the French invention 'staggered about 50 feet before collapsing and was never heard of again'. British sympathies are likely to lie with the Daimler claim. After all, the innovative spirit of the great man was fired by a visit to Britain during the industrial revolution in the 1860s, when he was a student engineer in Leeds and Manchester.

Animal Antics

. . . or all creatures great and small . . .

It's Not the Same Without the Girls

Dinosaurs may have vanished from the Earth simply because the last batch of young were all the same sex.

The theory springs from a discovery made about reptile eggs. If alligator eggs are hatched at a temperature above 34°C the babies are all males. But when the hatching is carried out at less than 30°C the babies are all females. The same experiment on another reptile, the turtle, gave a similar result, but the other way round.

Man Friday

A race-card for the Prix de L'Indre-et-Loire at Enghien in France showed that one of the horses was named Robinson Crusoe. The jockey was listed as M. Friday.

Taken to the Cleaners

Skin-diving biologists have now identified forty species of what are called cleaner fish. They pick off lice and other parasites from the bodies of other fish.

Cleaner fish don't usually travel about with their hosts. Instead they have stations among the rocks to which the customers go when they feel in need of a clean-up. Queues of fish line up in the vicinity of a station and as one satisfied customer swims away, the next fish moves in for treatment.

Cleaner fish – no matter how small – have no fear of being eaten by their customers – no matter how big. The little Red Sea wrasse, which is rarely longer than five millimetres, serves as cleaner to one of the most ferocious of all fish, the moray eel. When the wrasse has completed work on the outside of the eel, the host opens its terrifying jaws, and the little fish swim in to deal with the interior. While the wrasse is at work, the eel keeps its mouth wide open until its tiny partner has emerged.

Gardener's Nightmare

One word guaranteed to give gardeners nightmares is – aphids. When greenfly and blackfly – both aphids – appear on the roses and the runner beans, we reach for our spray guns. But it's no use; though gardeners and farmers destroy them, and birds and other insects devour them by the billion, aphids are the world's greatest survivors.

If the offspring of one aphid could reproduce for a single season without any interference, the progeny would be so numerous that the whole Earth would be covered with a solid layer of aphids.

Jungle Juice

Things can get out of hand in the South African jungle when elephants gorge themselves on the fermented fruit of the marula tree. The huge revellers become involved in noisy, drunken brawls, reeling about and falling over in futile attempts to charge one another.

Too Many Pigeon Pies

In the United States during the last century, there were times when the sun was darkened by vast flocks of passenger pigeons. One flock, which took three days to pass, is believed to have had more than 2,000 *million* birds in it.

Unfortunately for the passenger pigeon, it was very good to eat, and easy to kill or capture. By the beginning of the twentieth century the great flocks had all but vanished, and vain attempts were made to save the species.

In a zoo in Cincinnati in 1914, the last passenger pigeon in the world, whose name was Martha, died of old age.

Aerial Surveillance

When a man in Halifax, Yorkshire, goes for a drive in his car, his pet pigeon goes with him. Not in the car ... not on the car ... but a few feet higher than the car, and to the right of it. It's the ideal spot for keeping an eye on its owner.

A Good Wash with a Skeleton

What is a sponge – animal, vegetable or mineral?

At one time it was thought that sponges were plants but, in fact, they are animals. When they are brought out of the sea they still have flesh on them so they are left out in the sun until the flesh decays. The dead flesh is then washed off, and we scrub ourselves with the skeleton that remains.

. . . . . The insect population on 2.6 kilometres of land equals the total number of people on earth . . . .

Monster Eats Monster

The giant squid is often portrayed as a ferocious wrecker of ships and eater of people. Yet the biggest of these creatures, with tentacles as long as telephone poles and eyes the size of footballs, are really quite shy.

They live 200 to 400 metres below the surface and usually come up only when dead or dying. Much of their time is spent hiding from whales, who eat them whole. One giant squid, 12 metres long, was found intact – but very, very dead – in the stomach of a 70-tonne sperm whale.

Gotta Glow

Deep in the sunless depths of the ocean live a whole range of glow-in-the-dark creatures. One is the flashlight fish, which has no worries about ever needing new batteries – it gets its light from hitch-hiking bacteria.

Fish and bacteria exchange benefits. The fish offers the bacteria a reasonably safe home and a source of nutrients; the glowing bacteria provide the fish with light for luring other fish within striking range, communicating with fellow fish, or avoiding other fish that want to make a meal of it.

A Very Rich Diet!

Zoos always have problems supplying their animals with balanced diets but one Swedish zoo found itself with an embarrassment of riches . . .

One of the resident seals suffering from stomach ache was found to have swallowed 256 coins thrown into its pool by visitors.

TAKE 1
ALKA SELTZER
EVERY 10 COINS
ZOO DIRECTOR.

Disposable Spectacles

Having no eyelids, snakes cannot close their eyes. And a life-style of crawling on the ground means a great deal of dirt and grit in the eyes.

But snakes don't have to worry. Each time they shed their skin, the new one comes complete with a fresh pair of clear eye covers.

Guard and Guide Gander

An aged, blind woman in the United States had a gander that led her to church by taking the hem of her dress in its bill. During the service, the gander waited in a nearby cemetery, where it spent its time clipping the grass.

In Dumbarton, Scotland, a flock of 70 geese mounts guard over a distillery, where 115 million litres of whisky are stored. Trespassers are greeted by hissing, honking and sharp bites.

..... The ribbon worm doesn't have to worry about food shortages. It can eat up to 95% of its own body and still survive . . . .

Antique Feast in a Deep Freeze

One day the peasants of a small town in Siberia in 1901 could not understand why their dogs were so excited. They followed them out of town – and made a fascinating discovery. The dogs had dug up a mammoth in perfect condition which though partly covered by the frozen earth was just close enough to the surface to let the dogs have a sniff of the meat.

Although the last mammoth died about 10,000 years ago in the frozen wastes of northern Russia, it is not uncommon to find parts of the creatures preserved in the ice. But to find a complete body was unique.

Experts were summoned to deal with the huge elephant-like monster. The thick skin was carefully cut off and mounted, and the contents of the stomach examined. There was evidence still of the animal's last meal – thirteen kilogrammes of cones, flowers, moss and pieces of tree.

Fortunately, the finders of the treasure received their reward. The still-fresh meat was given to the dogs, and they feasted on it for days.

Tail-end of the Story

A tadpole loses its tail as it turns into a frog – but where does the tail go? Part is absorbed into the body as tissue and the rest is absorbed into the bloodstream.

Unfortunately, the change does not do much for the creature's character – it stops being a vegetarian and becomes a greedy carnivore – sometimes even cannibal – instead!

Let Youth Take Its Turn

People are not the only mammals that exploit their own kind. During an experiment, rats were trained to press a key that delivered some food. Someone had the bright idea of putting a young, untrained rat in with an older, trained rat. Would the older rat show the younger rat the ropes?

Over a period of time the recording instrument indicated that the key was being pressed more frequently than usual. The scientists went to the observation window to see what was happening.

The old rat was reclining in comfort under the food spout, while the younger one was pressing the key with youthful enthusiasm.

Head Down for the Iron-eater

The giant panda, which lives in the wild only in China, is described in an ancient book as an 'iron-eater'. Proof of the truth of this was provided recently when a keeper gave a panda a meal in an iron basin. The panda ate the food . . . and then, to the keeper's horror, the basin as well!

..... *The giraffe can kill most other animals by using its neck and head as a club* ....

Jilted Jumbo

For eighteen years Sandra, an Indian elephant, was looked after by her companion and trainer, Helmut Krone. But when the circus visited La Spezia, in Italy, Helmut fell in love with a pretty local girl. She did not care for the life of sawdust and so Helmut was forced to choose between her and the Big Top. The circus moved on without him.

Sandra protested by going on hunger strike. Vets from Paris to Milan did what they could, but even the honey they poured down her throat was rejected. Many attempts were made by the desperate circus owners to find Helmut, but he could not be traced. Broken-hearted, Sandra simply got thinner and thinner, and finally died.

HELMUT SAYS HE WISHES HIS OLD LADY WOULD GO ON HUNGER STRIKE!

Supreme Impression

The village hall committee at Wigginton in Yorkshire wanted a simple ceremony to open the rebuilt hall. The chairman of the committee insisted that they did not want lots of dignitaries.

So, the ceremony was performed by Mulgrove Supreme, a stud stallion owned by the Queen. He did the job by leaving an imprint of a hoof in the wet concrete.

Eat Dirt, Worm!

The solution to at least part of our rubbish problems may be — worms. In a test in Florida, 1.5 acres of worms consumed about 5 tonnes of waste — five times their own weight — in a single day.

Men Are All the Same

In the days of the Raj, a district officer in the Indian Civil Service was plagued with complaints from local farmers about bears damaging their crops. So he decided to shoot a bear to discourage the others.

Our hero took up a vantage point before dawn, but it was so cold that he could hardly feel the rifle. Then a large male bear appeared, followed by a female a few feet behind.

The officer tried to sight the quivering rifle, and fired. The bullet just nicked the male bear's backside. The animal stopped, sat down, and rubbed his rump. Then he gazed at his spouse, who was standing still, looking puzzled.

Arriving at the probable explanation, the male stood, cuffed the female firmly on the ear, and then continued on his way. The female, looking aggrieved, sat down and rubbed her head.

After a few moments, she ambled sadly after her mate, taking up her usual position a few feet behind him.

To Thine Own Dog Be True

A dog was put in kennels for a fortnight while husband and wife went on holiday. When they returned, the wife dropped off at the house to get on with the unpacking, while hubby drove over to the kennels.

The return journey home was something of a nightmare. The dog howled, yapped and barked, while the driver shouted, swore and threatened the animal with immediate extermination.

Back at the house, the husband complained bitterly: 'I can't imagine what they've done at those kennels! This dog's off its rocker! Perhaps he prefers it there. I don't know!'

'I do,' said his wife calmly. 'You see, you've got the wrong dog.'

Whose Side Are They On?

Laddie and Boy, two drug-detector dogs, just didn't have their hearts in their work. They were used by the drug squad in a raid in the Midlands in 1967. While a police officer was questioning two suspects, the offenders patted the dogs who responded by lying down and going to sleep.

But they woke up when the officer moved to arrest the suspects. One of the dogs growled at him, and the other leapt up and bit him. Laddie and Boy were given their cards.

Birdbrains

Do the animals we race for our amusement really want to race? The answer may lie in what happened in 1978 when 6,745 racing pigeons were released at Preston in Lancashire. A total of 5,545 were never seen again.

Experts have come up with two possible explanations. First, they flew over a grouse moor and were shot. But the secretary of the Ayrshire Federation of Homing Pigeons said, 'I can't believe they could have got all 5,545.' Second, the birds may simply have opted out, and gone to live by the seaside in Devon. And why not?

A Blessed Coupling

The Dean of Hereford Cathedral, a somewhat pompous cleric, decided to make his importance more public by riding a horse in front of a religious procession. So he mounted his mare, and opened his prayer book to show all and sundry the degree of his piety.

But a nearby stallion, unconcerned with the dean's dignity, had his own ideas. He broke loose, made for the mare and mounted her. The unfortunate dean was securely trapped while the stallion had his way.

It's a Dog's Life

TV personality Katie Boyle had a sticker on her car which read, 'Dogs Deserve Better People'.

While driving one day she noticed people pointing at the car and making agitated gestures. She stopped to investigate. Balanced precariously on top of the car roof was her Yorkshire terrier — sitting upright in its basket.

..... Owls have a reputation for being wise. The truth is that they have very small brains, and are among the least intelligent of birds. Crows and blue jays are among the most intelligent ....

Elephants Won't Work Overtime

The Burmese working elephant is a stickler for routine. It goes like this:

5 a.m.   Its oozie picks it up from the jungle, where it has been free all night, eating and sleeping. The oozie takes it to the river for a bath. This lasts an hour.

7 a.m.   Breakfast — a dish of steaming rice, and sometimes lentils. Then off to work which may be miles away.

9 a.m.   Begins work, dragging cut-down trees to the nearest river.

Noon   Rest for an hour.

1 p.m.   Resumes work.

4 p.m.   Stops work, whether the oozie says so or not. An elephant just won't work overtime. Back to the river for another bath.

6 p.m.   Supper. Usually mashed oatmeal with some bananas and coconuts. After supper, back to the jungle, where it completes its eating for the day — usually about 600lbs.

Ten Hens on the Richter Scale!

Earthquakes are still taking us by storm, but for animals they come as no great surprise.

In August 1979, 200 instruments along the Calaveres Fault in California failed to predict an earthquake so powerful that it shook San Francisco, 80 miles away. But in 1974, before a massive quake in China, snakes abandoned hibernation and crawled out of the ground, pigs climbed walls, hens would not go to roost, and trained German Shepherd dogs refused to obey their owners. The Chinese heeded these warnings, evacuated the area, and hundreds of thousands of people were saved.

The Hunter Who Failed to Duck

A New Zealander who went duck shooting is wondering if he should wear a crash helmet next time. The hunter blasted his shotgun at a duck, missing with both barrels. The quarry decided to counter-attack, circled its target, and dive-bombed with deadly accuracy into the hunter's face.

Damage – a broken nose, glasses and one tooth.

. . . . . The horsefly has a cutting tool like a pointed rod that it drives up and down to drill into its victim's skin. Once the wound has been made, the horsefly plunges a tube into it and takes a long, warm drink. . . . .

Big Job

News of old boys in a Shropshire school magazine: 'After a spell at chicken farming Peter has been engaged by a carpet company to cover Lancashire and Cheshire.'

You Get Up My Nose, Darling!

The anglerfish is so named because of the way it catches its food. It uses a rod and line technique, the rods being spines on the back fins. As the anglerfish lives in the darkness of the deep seas, it has a light organ at the ends of the rods. To attract other fish, it waves the rods about, and then snaps up the prey when it comes within striking distance.

The female anglerfish weighs up to half a tonne. The male, which is only a few millimetres long, spends almost its entire life attached to its spouse's nose.

Put Down

A middle-aged woman on the train to Winchester had been trying for some time to quieten her small dog which was yapping and snarling at an elderly man opposite.

'Boysie usually has such a sweet nature,' she sighed. 'I just don't know what to make of him.'

The man peered over his glasses at the animal. 'Well,' he suggested, 'how about a nice rug?'

Beware of the Dog

Like most south coast towns, Budleigh Salterton, Devon, has a high proportion of the elderly and infirm among its population – animal, as well as human. But their needs are borne in mind. A holiday visitor reports seeing this sign in a narrow lane off the Exmouth road: 'Please drive slowly – dog is deaf.'

A museum whose stuffed exhibits include a lamb with four eyes and a pig with two faces was up for sale at Arundel, Sussex, price £340,000.

Ferreted Out

One of the biggest of the North Sea oil platforms in the deepest water had an intractable problem. It was necessary to link the underwater well-head to the platform above by an electric cable. The two were already connected by a pipe, but none of the experts could find a way of coaxing a cable through the pipe.

A ferret handler was called in and he arrived from Scotland with two ferrets and a dead rabbit. The rabbit was blown through the pipework by means of a compressor. Then the ferret was allowed after it, wearing a harness and pulling a thin line. The ferret followed the trail of the rabbit to the sea-bed and back and the cable was pulled through after it.

. . . . . *Millions of years ago, the plains of North America were inhabited by herds of camels, about the size of a sheep* . . . .

. . . . . *In a single day, a black widow spider has been known to devour twenty husbands* . . . .

Keeping Up with Consumer Demand

The only answer for a species that gets eaten in huge quantities is to produce enough young to keep ahead of the appetites of the carnivores.

This compensation by nature leads to some spectacular numbers in the undersea world where open, hungry mouths are the order of the day. The oyster keeps ahead of consumer demand by laying 60 million eggs a year, and the turbot between 8 and 14 million. The plaice manages 300,000, and the sole 130,000, while the herring manages to keep the species going with a mere 40,000.

Significantly, the elephant, which is rarely eaten, hardly ever even produces twins.

..... *Women are better than men when it comes to teaching a budgie to talk. The birds find it easier to imitate a high-pitched voice* ....

A R.I.P.-off

The antics of most animals are as nothing compared with the antics of humans about their animal pets.

The Hartsdale Canine Cemetery in Westchester, USA, has more than just dogs interred there. The 40,000 laid-to-rest pets include goldfish, cats, parrots, monkeys, salamanders and even a lion.

One lady has lashed out for 58 top-pet funerals, including those for a piglet and a bantam rooster. One dog, said to be a war hero, is buried in a major's uniform.

On a fine Sunday, at least 100 people turn up, and spend the day visiting the graves of their departed pets. One woman, who turns up twice a week, takes off her shoes before entering the cemetery, as a tribute to her late dog.

Plots cost about $500.

..... *Each day, just to live, the shrew has to eat its own weight in food. If it eats nothing for two hours it dies* ....

There's No Business

DOUBLE YOLKS

. . . or the show must go on . . .

Monopoly Money

Dynasty star George Hamilton surprised friends at his home when he played 'Monopoly' – using $10,000 in genuine $1, $5, $10, $20, $50 and $100 bills. He wanted to make the game more exciting. But when it was over, George made the winner hand the money back. Good game, eh!

Cheque-mate

Soul singer Gladys Knight couldn't get a Beverly Hills shop-girl to cash a cheque, even though she insisted she was a big star and good for the money. Finally to prove the point she broke into a rendition of her hit 'Midnight Train to Georgia'. That did the trick and the girl accepted her cheque.

. . . . . When the TV serial 'Dynasty' was at the height of its popularity, Joan Collins was receiving 12,000 fan letters a week . . . .

Shall I Take Your Sausages, Sir?

When David Niven was a young officer in the Regular Army, he was invited to a fancy dress ball at a grand house in Leicestershire. Determined to impress, he went as a clown, complete with pompoms, a string of sausages, a long false nose and all the trimmings.

David arrived early, anxious to meet all the important people he knew would be there. There was just a flicker of surprise on the butler's face as he ushered him into the drawing-room. It was certainly full of smart people – but all of them were in full evening dress. David had got the date right but the month wrong.

And the host and hostess thought they were being kind and thoughtful when they invited him to stay for dinner.

Second to None

In a recent competition for choirs in Wales, there was only one entry, and even then it didn't manage to win. The adjudicators listened to the choir and announced their decision. The choir was placed second as a penalty for turning up late.

..... The longest kiss in cinema history was the marathon of 185 seconds by Regis Toomey and Jane Wyman – who later became Mrs Ronald Reagan! ....

Walkies in the Valley

Jayne Mansfield won the heart of the British public in 1967 when she tried to smuggle her two chihuahuas into the country under her fur coat. Clutching the two tiny dogs to her famous bosom, she appeared in the papers with the caption, 'I am animal crackers! I have had chihuahuas ever since I was a little girl. They are so dependent . . . they appeal to my mother instinct!'

Sing Something Simple

TV personality Dickie Henderson had a reputation for putting his foot in it. Sometimes he did even better than that. He put both feet in . . .

He was once at a big showbusiness party, during which a woman with an awful voice began to sing. Dickie turned to a man near him and told him what he thought of the turn.

Instead of agreeing, the man replied, 'I think I should tell you, the lady is my wife.'

Covering up desperately, Dickie said, 'Oh, it's not her fault. It's the song – it's dreadful!'

The man replied coldly, 'Do you think so? I wrote it.'

WE'LL GET A GOOD CROWD TOMORROW FOR THE BOTTOM HALF!

Not the Right Calibre?

The trouble with 'Rita Thunderbird' may have been that she didn't stick to her diet. Anyway, as cannon fodder she failed miserably on two occasions, getting firmly stuck in the weapon, instead of sailing gracefully out of its mouth in her gold lamé bikini.

One of these attempts was marginally successful. Although 'Rita' got stuck in the cannon, her bra didn't. It sailed, without 'Rita' in it, across the River Thames.

A Record Failure

The Norwegian entry for the 1978 Eurovision song contest was a number called 'Mile After Mile'. It was so unbelievably dreary that the voting from panels all over Europe was unanimous: 'Norway – no points'. This was a record that pushed even the winner, Izhar Cohen, out of the picture. Press photographers queued up to get a shot of the Norwegian pop star Jan Teigain. He was showered with offers of tours, TV appearances and radio interviews.

What a Choker

A pantomime Dick Whittington turned to an old showbiz remedy to cure a sore throat when Amanda Noar tried to restore her singing voice by gargling with port wine. But the croaky star swallowed some of the remedy — and later failed a breath test.

In court her lawyer explained, 'In addition to normal medication, Amanda resorted to something which is part of theatre folklore.' But the judge wasn't so sure, and fined her £200.

Bless This House

Harry Secombe's visit to Pentonville Prison may have been intended to provide a little innocent escapism for the inmates, but one song didn't go down as well as he'd hoped. It was 'Bless this house', which includes the lines: 'Bless these walls so firm and stout, Keeping strife and trouble out. . . '

. . . . . *A music critic wrote: 'An amateur string quartet played Brahms here last evening. Brahms lost.'* . . . .

Never To Be Repeated

At rehearsal, aerialist Tito Gaona had brought off the impossible: he had performed the first ever quadruple somersault from a flying trapeze 60 feet above the ground. When the circus came to New York in 1978, Tito was there as the star attraction. Confident publicity posters proclaimed: 'Can aerialist Tito Gaona — spinning at 75 miles an hour — accomplish the most difficult acrobatic feat of the twentieth century?'

The thousands who rolled up did not expect the answer to be 'No'. Every night for nine months poor Tito missed his catcher and plummeted into the safety net.

'Just Like That!'

The amateur magician was nervous when he made his first public appearance at the age of 17. From the beginning everything went wrong. For a start he forgot his patter. When he opened his mouth he couldn't think of anything to say, so he closed it again.

Then the tricks went haywire. He either made them obvious, or they didn't work at all. The audience watched spellbound. They'd never seen anything like it.

Then he came to his big finale. He produced a bottle of milk and placed paper over the top. In a shaking voice he told the audience, 'I shall turn the bottle upside down and take the paper away. The milk will stay in the bottle.'

The magician turned the bottle, paused, and took the paper away. The milk cascaded down his trousers. The magician felt that something needed to be said. He opened his mouth, but nothing came out. Sweating heavily and trembling, he tottered from the stage. He stood swaying in the wings, listening to the audience – cheering wildly.

Tommy Cooper's career had begun.

No Motion Replay

People in show business must have quite a job remembering who's married to who at any given moment. Billie Whitelaw, the actress, found herself in just that kind of trouble.

She was at a lunch given by the Variety Club of Great Britain. Billie was talking to a well-known actor who was recently divorced. Deciding he needed a lift, Billie said, 'There's a good friend of mine across the room. I'm sure you'll get on just fine. Come and meet her.'

A deathly silence greeted the introduction and only then did Billie realize that she'd introduced the actor to his ex-wife.

Critics Get the Bird

Never in the history of television entertainment has there been such a clash between critics and public as there was in 1984 over the blockbuster *Thorn Birds*.

The critics:

'I didn't realize it was a comedy show. Monday's episode was hilarious.' *Daily Star*

'The only things wrong with *Thorn Birds* are the story, the script, the acting, the settings and the pace. Apart from that, it's great.' *Daily Mirror*

'Tepid – another *Dallas*, only with more funerals.' *Daily Express*

The public:

One episode had more viewers than the Royal Wedding. So many people switched on – 22 million – that an extra power station had to be brought into operation.

. . . . . *Glasgow graffito: 'Listening to the bagpipes is a fate worse than deaf.'* . . . .

Farce of a Festival

David Garrick, the famous 18th century actor-manager, was responsible for organizing a Shakespeare Centenary Festival. Unfortunately, everything seemed to go wrong.

First of all, he laid it on in 1769, which was five years late, and in the wrong month. Then on the appointed day it rained very heavily, causing all the fireworks to fail to light. And to crown it all, a wall collapsed, injuring an honoured guest.

Plus ça Change?

Do people who make TV documentaries really have their heart in their work? A BBC crew made a series in Sierra Leone, in Africa. A number of extras were employed, and the going rate for whites was five times that for blacks.

The series? 'The Fight Against Slavery.'

An Initials Error

Magnus Magnusson of *Mastermind* would have done well to say 'Pass' when he went to make a documentary programme with archaeological excavators in Dover.

He reported the discovery of evidence that Dover had been the headquarters of the Roman fleet (*Classis Britannicus*), and that the chief evidence for this was a slate with the Roman initials C.B. inscribed on it. The slate was handed with great care to Magnus, so that he could hold it up for the cameras. Instead – he dropped it.

The fracture went straight across the precious initials.

Softly, Softly, George

George Cole, the actor who made his name in television's *Minder*, was once appearing in a play with the famous character actor, Alastair Sim. On one disastrous evening George made a bad-tempered exit from the stage and took with him the door handle. Which left Alastair Sim stranded without any obvious way of making his own exit.

After the show, George was driving the irate Alastair home, and received a lecture on the desirability of acting properly and controlling his strength. Somewhat upset, George changed gear with unnecessary violence, only to find that the gear lever had come away in his hand.

He handed it to Alastair and they walked home.

Musical Pigs

Louis XI of France once ordered one of his abbots to invent a ridiculous musical instrument for the amusement of the court. The abbot met the challenge by assembling a line of pigs. The squeal of each pig had a distinctive pitch and by pricking each of them in a particular order, the abbot was able to play a tune.

The Bridle Path

When Peter Sellers was a young actor, he met a girl at a dance and asked if he might take her home. It was a beautiful evening and so he suggested that they should walk along the bridle path.

The young lady's response? 'Oh, Peter, don't you think it's a little early to think of getting married?'

. . . . . The Decca recording company refused to contract the Beatles because they thought they were too old-fashioned . . . . . .

Better Late than Never

Juan Potomachi, a wealthy Argentinian businessman, revealed his secret ambition when his will was published in 1955. Part of it read:

'All my life I wanted to be on the stage. I leave 200,000 pesos to a fund from which talented young actors shall get yearly scholarships. My only condition is that my head be preserved and used as the skull in *Hamlet*.'

Pass the Porter

It's not often that an opera singer manages to knock back a pint of porter on stage when she's meant to be dying of thirst in a desert. Nevertheless, Maria Milbran managed it every night during the run of *The Maid of Artois* at Drury Lane.

In the last act, as she sank exhausted behind a pile of drifted sand in the desert, a pint of welcome refreshment was slipped through a small gap in the scenery.

Minutes later, fully fortified, Maria rose to electrify the audience with a final burst of song.

In Limbo

At a performance of Gounod's famous opera *Faust*, the trap-door leading to the nether regions stuck, allowing only the lower half of Mephistopheles to disappear.

There was an awkward pause on the stage, and then a voice rang out from the gallery, 'See that, lads, hell's full!'

A Right Royal Welcome

Usually the BBC can be relied upon to come up with just the right sound effect for any occasion. But the introduction provided for the broadcast by the King of Norway was . . . well . . . not absolutely on the right note.

The effects department had been asked for a fanfare, but someone read the order as 'funfair'. So, the King's speech was introduced by, 'Roll up! Roll up! All the fun of the fair', with a barrel organ playing, 'Over the waves'.

. . . . . *John Barrymore holds the world record for the number of kisses delivered in a single film. In* Don Juan *he kissed at the rate of one every 53 seconds, making a grand total of 191 kisses* . . . . . .

All Right, I'm Going

It happened during a performance of Shakespeare's immortal play *Antony and Cleopatra* at Stratford-upon-Avon. Defeated in battle, Antony began to disrobe in preparation for his suicide.

'Off, pluck off,' he says, giving a servant the cue to remove his cloak.

But on this night the actor playing the servant didn't respond. He was obviously miles away, oblivious of his surroundings. 'Pluck off,' Antony repeated but there was still no response.

Desperate, the anxious hero said the line once more, this time in a loud and firm voice. The servant came to, looked offended and stalked off the stage.

It is said that he has since changed his profession.

Why must the show go on . . .

Alan Devlin is one actor who does not believe that 'the show must go on'. The occasion was a performance of HMS *Pinafore* at Dublin's Gaiety Theatre. Mr Devlin was in the middle of 'I am the ruler of the King's navee', when he decided he had better things to do.

He shouted out, 'Blow this for a game of soldiers,' and announced that he was leaving. Then he simply walked off the stage – leaving the chorus dumbfounded.

. . . and on

That wasn't the first time Alan Devlin had gone AWOL on stage. Nor the second. Nor, indeed, the third. When asked why he did it, he said honestly: 'The world and his wife know why I do it. I do it because I'm drunk.'

. . . . . On the tombstone of the film comedian, W. C. Fields, are the words: 'On the whole, I'd rather be in Philadelphia.' . . . .

The Martians are Coming

One of the most notorious moments in radio broadcasting happened in America in 1938.

It occurred during an adaptation of *The War of the Worlds*, H. G. Wells's futuristic novel about an invasion from Mars. The presenter was Orson Welles, and before the programme began assurances were given that this was fiction not fact.

Nevertheless, so realistic was Welles's reading that the people who switched on once the broadcast had begun were convinced that a Martian invasion had indeed begun. Some families even fled their homes to the safety of the countryside.